THE FREEDOM TO BE FREE

THE FREEDOM TO BE FREE

James Marshall

The John Day Company

NEW YORK

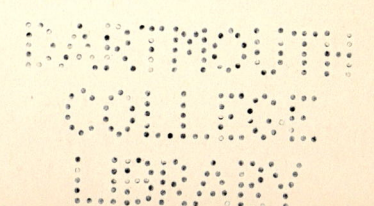

COPYRIGHT, 1941, 1942, 1943, BY JAMES MARSHALL

All rights reserved. This book, or parts thereof, must not be reproduced in any form without permission.

MANUFACTURED IN THE UNITED STATES OF AMERICA

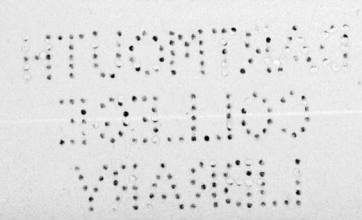

To
JUDAH L. MAGNES
AND
IRWIN EDMAN

Contents

Foreword   1

Part I—Revolution Against Paternalism

1. We Don't Know a Revolution When We See One   13
2. Liberty, Equality and Fraternity   37
3. Competitive Society   60

Part II—Some Problems of Democracy

4. What Is This Thing Democracy?   81
5. Doctor, Mammoth and Co-operative Society   105
6. Wayward Nations   142
7. International Democracy and Biting off More Than One Can Chew   181

Part III—The Propagation of the Faith

8. Plato's Sea Captain and Buddha's Navel   223
9. Man Cannot Live by Words Alone   247

Index   273

Foreword

MEDICINE IS A SCIENCE so flexible that it is a matter for levity that the food which would poison the baby a generation ago is now basic to the baby's nutrition. When Newton's theory of gravity failed to explain the bending rays of starlight, the theory was modified, even though the classical assumptions of Euclid had to be suspended in part.

This impersonal modesty of the scientists has made possible the progress since Descartes, and as by-products has produced mechanical invention and the means for a surplus economy, has lengthened the span of life and has added all the gruesome gadgets of war.

In *Experimental Medicine* Claude Bernard says, discussing science: "The ideas and theories of our predecessors must be preserved only in so far as they represent the present state of science, but they are obviously destined to change, unless we admit that science is to make no further progress, and that is impossible. . . . As truths in the experimental sciences—are only relative, these sciences can move forward only by revolution and by recasting old truths in a new scientific form."

Are not the truths of social science also relative?

In politics and other human relations, we are far less willing than in science to substitute new ideas for old. It is easier for the mathematician to abandon the Euclidean hypothesis that two parallel lines will remain parallel into infinite space than it is for men in power to concede that power which is concentrated becomes corrupt.

The facts that one man's pleasure is another's pain, and that the practitioner of politics or industry is influenced by rewards and punishments, make the acceptance of objective truth difficult. The political animal, man, is forever fearful of being starved or burned or emasculated. Consequently, the acceptance of a new ideology and the abandonment of old theory are scarcely to be anticipated without struggles in which the issues become lost in rhetoric and passion and fear. The issues become divorced from the problems to be solved. In a lather of confusion, we lose sight of our moral ends and forget the original stimulus.

When we do discuss the social science field in a logical manner, we are apt to think that we can prove all of our allegations. Actually, just as in the physical sciences we are making certain fundamental suppositions—that human nature does not change, that self-interest is the greatest incentive, or that the most important thing in life on earth is to prepare for a life hereafter.

Such assumptions involve an acceptance of the *status quo* of man's surrender to anxieties and terrors and the inevitability of his domination by men possessed of greater power or authority. But there is a parallel instinctual urge in man, a constructive urge, to achieve what we loosely call "freedom." Louis Fischer quotes Gandhi as inquiring whether President Roosevelt's four freedoms include "the freedom to be free." We may well paraphrase the question by asking whether any given political, economic or social institution or formula offers men the freedom to be free. This is the great question. It is the yardstick of man's

Foreword

progress. What political and economic institutions tend to free men from the dominion of others, and which do not? What attitudes, what approaches, what relationships tend to free men from anxiety and terror and their resulting drives of hatred and destruction?

In the search for the freedom to be free there has grown up through centuries a formula which we call democracy. It is expressed in an agglomeration of slogans and institutions, partially tried out, partially successful, shot through with tracer bullets and fragments of older, authoritarian formulae. How and why is the democratic principle relevant to being free?

Quite consciously, I shall here make certain assumptions about what the democratic principle involves, as follows:

1. Respect for individuals and the variations among individuals, their needs and their aspirations,

2. Making possible equal opportunity for every individual to obtain satisfaction by realizing and expressing his capacities and pursuing his interests,

3. Equality of treatment of each individual by those with power or authority,

4. The concept that equality does not mean identity but a recognition of differences, a recognition of differences not in the form of favoritism but as an expression of respect for individuality,

5. Collaboration, rather than competition or paternalism, as the more likely method for achieving mutual respect, equality and development.

Although the social sciences are concerned with human beings and their attitudes and relations to one another, they have paid scant attention to human behavior. They have not given a place of importance to psychology, the science of human behavior, though practitioners of medicine, education and social work have incorporated many of its findings in their day-to-day procedures. Historian, economist, sociologist and political scientist have looked to the gods, to climate, to the means of production, to heredity and to the whims of important persons for laws and explanations of social behavior. But usually the primary human motives and the effect of group environment upon them have been ignored.

What has made history is not wet and cold, public or private ownership, white skins or large bodies, the anger of Thor or the fair face of Helen of Troy, but the hopes and anxieties, the aggression and fraternity, the logical plans and the spontaneous outbursts which have been set off or played upon by those other influences. Except in romantic versions of history, we have tended to ignore psychological drives, to look for external causes and to be satisfied by them. Then we wonder why the lessons of history are not learned. We paint the walls of our world with ideological murals. Then we wonder why they have no depth and seem at times scarcely to touch us.

It is because we disregard the grim psychological dialectic, the unspoken conflicts and unresolved impulses behind human behavior, that we find ourselves deceived so often. We are deceived by others less deeply than by ourselves for our readiness to avoid the application of psychological science to the material of the social sciences.

"Always and everywhere," Henry Adams wrote, "the mind creates its own universe, and pursues its own

Foreword

phantoms; but the force behind the image is always a reality. . . ." Behind many an image lies the reality of insecurity. Out of our anxieties we create universes to be roamed and phantoms to be pursued.

So in our insecurity we try to find scapegoats and sedatives. We speak of foreign things, of totalitarian government, of enemy nations, as a danger or a threat to our democracy. And though the triumph of their arms would indeed be the destruction of our democracy, we have a tendency to blame our shortcomings and failures on totalitarian states and to evade our own responsibility for the development of our own democracy. "The serious threat to our democracy is not the existence of foreign totalitarian states. It is the existence within our own personal attitudes and within our own institutions of conditions similar to those which have given a victory to external authority, discipline, uniformity, and dependence upon The Leader in foreign countries. The battlefield is also accordingly here —within ourselves and our institutions," John Dewey wrote in *Freedom and Culture*.

American democracy and democratic institutions do not depend for survival on anthems or flags or shouts of patriotism. They are not to be assured by the victories of war or the councils of leagues of nations. Their survival can only be assured by a wholehearted respect for a democratic idealism which is understood in its historical and psychological settings, and by a courageous intelligence which is prepared to adjust those ideals to current situations, even though it entails abandonment of once serviceable fictions and institutions.

We are inclined to find in science, too, a sedative to our

uncertainty. We feel assurance in the electric eye, the conquest of the stratosphere, the sulfa drugs. We accept in these a wizardry that seems endless, miracles as satisfying as those performed by a saint. But increased knowledge and control of the physical world have not always produced satisfaction of human needs. The destruction has at least balanced the progress and security offered by physical science. Nothing in the greater knowledge of human nature or the practices and institutions of men will of itself assure a constructive application of such knowledge. Indeed, the abuses of propaganda have neutralized the benefits of modern psychological and psychiatric knowledge. It is not little knowledge that is the dangerous thing, but any knowledge which is unrelated to ethical ends.

Even our political advancement, the great slogans and institutions developed in France and Great Britain and America since the seventeenth century, must not lull us into a feeling that if only they were worldwide all would be well. Freedom in thought and in religious practice, freedom from the tyranny of princes, freedom of verbal expression, have not of themselves brought individual freedom. Nor can dialectical materialism offer more. Its aims are immersed in fatalism and its instruments have been destructive of human dignity. Marxism has magnified the importance of the means of production and their control; it also has ignored those psychological factors which make the needs of production important and stimulate the struggle for control.

The fundamental question is not one of power or of who possesses power, but of the ends of power and the uses to which power is to be put. Even the magnitude of power is

Foreword

important only as compared to the magnitude of possible restraining forces. Yet, if we could conceive of political power not as necessarily controlled by opposition, but as constructively canalized—as a thunderbolt guided in a laboratory rather than lightning striking from the clouds—power would be less of a threat, of less concern in our lives and to our social organizations.

The primary problem, then, is one of uses and ends. It is a problem at once ethical and psychological. The knowledge that in most people, even in powerful persons, there may be occurring a frenzied struggle for security, illuminates passages in political and economic concepts and helps us handle power conflicts. The fact that even the most able person may have fantastic misconceptions of his own capacities will explain many an illogical quest for satisfaction. Proving oneself, demonstrating potency, aggression, psychic cannibalism, these are factors in human relations which defeat the achievement of our ethical purposes, because they defeat the very satisfaction which they are aimed to achieve.

The failure to find satisfaction because of irrelevant cross-currents of emotion is illustrated in the play *Golden Boy*, by Clifford Odets. Tokio, the trainer of prize-fighters, says to Joe, the fighter, "Joe, you're loaded with love. Find something to give it to. Your heart ain't in fighting. . . . Your *hate* is. But a man with hate and nothing else . . . . he's half a man . . . . and a half a man . . . . is no man."

We can all find in our lives, if we dare to think deeply, examples of how we did not enjoy being with people we loved, or doing things we usually found pleasant, or eating a meal of our favorite dishes, simply because we were angry at someone who was not even present or because we feared something that might never come about.

Men or peoples may do things well, yet somehow never attain their ends, never achieve satisfactions, if they act in hate or in aggression or to reassure themselves that they are not inadequate. Hitler found an answering hatred, a hatred in his people which he could rouse and merge with his own. But would anyone claim that either he or the German people have found satisfaction in the instruments and expressions of this hatred? Stalin found in the Russian people a fear of outside interference equal to his own and answering to his own fears; but is there anything to show that either he or his people have found security or satisfaction in the aggressions and hates prompted by those fears? Japanese military leaders found in the Japanese people a common need for self-justification in a world in which dominant white races held yellow men to be a peril, discriminated against them and exploited them. But here again, neither the army of Japan nor the people of Japan have found satisfaction.

Nor have the democracies utilized their energies much better. The British and ourselves have chased the almighty dollar, idolized Sterling, and told and retold the fairy tale of the white man's burden, in order to give expression to our own aggressive instincts and our need of self-justification. But, the power struggles within and without our democracies have been too urgent and restless to let us find satisfaction.

Beginning, then, with the assumptions I have made concerning some of the elements of the democratic principle, let us look at our society with its confusion of moral ends and its psychological drives. Let us see if we can find what ends and attitudes can bring about a better realization of the democratic principle, and how we can go about the propagation of the democratic faith.

Part I
Revolution Against Paternalism

I

We Don't Know a Revolution When We See One

JOSHUA PERKINS came into his living room where his children were doing their homework. He called to the kitchen, "I'm home, Mother," greeted his son, kissed his daughter and sat down on the upholstered rocker that had belonged to his own mother.

"What are you studying today?" he asked his son.

"Labor economics—the Wagner act and minimum wage laws," Junior answered.

"When I was a boy we didn't read things like that. We studied Latin. Latin develops the mind," Perkins said. "And you?" he asked his daughter.

"I'm studying household economics," she replied.

Mr. Perkins snorted. "When I was a boy, girls learned such things in their mother's kitchen."

"Times have changed," the young people told him.

"I didn't gad about to the movies either. I worked for my father after school and Saturdays. And I didn't pretend to study with the radio going all the time."

"You don't understand the younger generation," his daughter said.

"You read your newspaper to the radio. You read about the war and the business page to the best swing bands," Junior informed him.

"That's different. I don't have to think for that," Mr. Perkins remarked.

The doorbell rang, and he went to the door. They could hear him talking guardedly to a man. Then they heard him say, "Nonsense. The last offer was five thousand"; and he swore and slammed the door.

Mrs. Perkins came to the hall. "What do you think? I was offered $1,500 for this house. Five years ago I had an offer of $5,000. Johnson's house sold for that."

"The neighborhood's changed. We should have moved then too," Mrs. Perkins said.

"Pull up roots!" he exclaimed.

"The Johnsons say the street is down at the heel," Junior told him.

The neighborhood had changed. The corner grocery and drug stores had given way to chain stores. Neighbors whom the Perkinses had known for years moved out and new ones came in. Several years ago a boardinghouse had been opened across the street. The boarders weren't all such nice people either. Next door a small apartment house had been built, covering the old front yard and back garden. Mr. and Mrs. Perkins still called the house on the other side "Johnsons'" but the Cellas had lived in it a few years and now they shared it with the Matcheks. The friends the Perkinses used to meet at church had moved away, and the congregation had changed. The taxes were no less, but now the old land value was gone—$1,500, when the last offer had been $5,000. It was hard to face these changes, hard to move away because of all the economic, emotional and social adjustments involved. Perkins couldn't see the neighborhood going down at the heel. He had been hoping against hope. He was still saying, "When I was a boy." The changes at any one time seemed slight. Life in America seemed stable, much as it had been before.

It is difficult to appreciate when a revolution is in progress. Its gradual approach and unfolding is like the change in Joshua Perkins's block. There are so many things the same; there are so many economic, emotional and social readjustments to be made in giving up the days "when I was a boy," as a norm for the measurement of what is satisfactory and right and, in fact, realizing and accepting that those days are gone beyond recall.

Until December 7, 1941, life in America had been going on much as it had for two decades, in spite of a world war and immense defensive efforts. Now we are inclined to regard such changes as are daily occurring as though they had a terminal date with the end of the war, as if control of production and consumption had no ancestry in such things as control of farm production and stock markets and would have no progeny in a national planning. It is not easy to realize, therefore, that we are living in a world in revolution; that actually this revolution is taking place in the United States as well as in Europe and Asia. Although we have means of communication and facilities of education which the *muzhik* of Russia and the *fellah* of Syria did not have in the late eighteenth or early nineteenth centuries, nevertheless our appreciation of the trends and the dynamics of the current revolution is little, if any, greater than was their comprehension of those movements which engrossed Washington and Jefferson, Montesquieu and Robespierre. We can envisage the fact that revolutions have occurred in Germany, Italy, Russia and China—perhaps even that France is in revolution; but the fact that there has been no change in the forms and little change in the personnel of government in Great Britain and the United States makes the concept of revolution in these countries seem unreal.

Revolution seems far away to us because we associate the word mostly with violence, and especially violence applied to a change in the form or personnel of government. We think in terms of the phrase "bloody revolution," and our imaginations are caught by the word "bloody" and do not proceed to recognition of the word "revolution." Our well-repressed primitive desire to spill blood is decorously satisfied by blood-and-thunder tales of heads on the guillotine. Economic theory and historical consequences unadorned by gun shots and boudoirs bore us. So we do not readily see those social changes in habit and practice, those economic differences in the supply and distribution of goods, those political variations in control and attitude, which occur with little fanfare but effectively change the relations of persons and groups. These changes and differences and variations are the body of the document of revolution to which the changes in government are only the signature and seal, a signature and seal necessitated only where a recognition of the facts is refused.

No one would question the revolutionary character of the abolition of private property rights, the creation of state capitalism and the collectivization of agriculture and industry in Soviet Russia. Few would deny the revolutionary character of the totalitarian concept of government, of the corporative state of Italy and the concept of single party control in the totalitarian states. Few would question the revolutionary nature of the control of labor, management and profits, the uses to which private property can be put and the congealing of labor fluidity in Germany, Russia and France today. Yet in the last decade, we in America have moved in many respects along parallel lines, and where those parallel lines diverge, it is largely due to the principles and practices which we call democracy.

When we see our high school graduation picture of twenty or thirty years ago, we may be shocked or amused, but we recognize some drastic changes in ourselves and our wives and our friends. If we could see as graphically the social, political and economic changes that have occurred in the same period, they would seem even more extreme. Compare, for example, the power and importance of the financier in the life of the United States and Great Britain prior to 1929 with his place in our economic life today. Not only has the contraction of financing caused by the depression restricted Wall Street and the City of London, but legislation has controlled stock exchanges and produce exchanges, has created commissions, such as the Securities Exchange Commission, which watch the *bona fides* and reduce the profits on private financing, and has limited the uses and changed the value of money. Governments have withdrawn gold itself, the commodity in which bankers dealt.

Through its loan and credit agencies, the government has in large measure replaced the private financier. It finances railroads, pipelines, factories and foreign trade in place of J. P. Morgan and Company and the other houses that underwrote securities. It lends money and guarantees loans to construct homes, performing the work and taking the risks of the savings banks.

In the field of labor, the Wagner Act and its creation, the Labor Relations Board, have granted greater power to labor organizations and strengthened the morale of organized labor. Bargaining between employer and employee is no longer optional; it is mandatory. The Norris-LaGuardia Act has reduced the power of the courts as an instrument for the suppression of strikes. The Wages and Hours Law has reversed almost two centuries of doctrine that labor is a product to be bartered and sold in competition. It revives in part the old statutes which eighteenth-century liberalism combated and which fixed the rates of wages to be paid to workers. When the British statute of laborers was repealed, it was revolutionary; our new Wages and Hours Law is no less so.

The government has taken control of agricultural production through loans and crop allotments; it limits or encourages the amount of grain to be grown and indirectly the amount of meat to be produced; and a farmer who exceeds his allotment cannot dispose of his produce. It is revolutionary that men who were formerly controlled by markets after the event are now controlled by government planning before they put the seed in the ground.

The wartime income and corporation taxes of Great Britain and the United States make the accumulation of wealth almost impossible. The wartime inheritance taxes will reduce to a small proportion fortunes which they touch. If such taxes continue for a generation—and they seem likely to remain in substance, though they will be modified after the war—the rich magnate so dear to the pens of cartoonists and the tongues of rabble rousers will have passed completely from the scene.

Even before the war program necessitated priorities and price regulation, we were moving toward a planned economy; we were headed in a direction which reversed the trend of liberalism and its inherent principle of free competition; we were acknowledging that free competition was meaningless in situations involving monopoly and was a free pass to suicide to agricultural and other small producers.

Freedom of contract reached its heights of unrealistic absurdity in decisions of the Supreme Court which forbade the government to interfere with minimum wages and child labor on the ground that the unorganized hungry were fit competitors for those who controlled the factories, the wages and the working conditions. But in recent years the Supreme Court has had to bring its formulae for the preservation of free contract and competition into line with the move toward planned economy. It has gone so far as to approve control of prices—the heart of free contract and competition—where "the economic maladjustment is one of price, which threatens harm to the producer at one end of the series and the consumer at the other." The court has indorsed the power of legislation to correct industrial practices which "make unrestricted competition an inadequate safeguard of the consumer's interests, produce waste harmful to the public, threaten ultimately to cut off the supply of a commodity needed by the public or portend the destruction of the industry itself. . . ."

We have not merely reversed the economic ideology of the eighteenth and nineteenth centuries; we have created the instruments to effectuate the new socialized ideology, and we have not stopped. Curiously enough, the first great American instrument for this end was created for another purpose. The Reconstruction Finance Corporation was organized by President Hoover to stem the deflationary movement of the depression insofar as it affected the corporate capital structure of basic industries. It has now become the successor to the great Wall Street banking houses as the source of industrial capital.

Not only the economic changes are important and revolutionary in their nature; but also the social changes. The move of young people from the country to the factory town means, among other things, working for cash and not for produce; it means being cogs in machines, in contrast to being individuals working more at their own tempo. It means changes in transportation, in amusements, in social habits, the kind of thing one hears and sees, the tempo of work and play. Nor has this movement ceased. The program of war industries has revived the citifying of the farm boy. In work and in play our mechanized age has tended to make American youth sedentary. It has exalted the sitting posture over the standing and the walking, over the use of mind and hand.

Furthermore, city life and recreation in cities have been impersonalized. Neighborliness, with its opportunities for common participation in the problems and pleasures of living, has lost its importance, and the values of shared pleasures have been reduced to holding hands at the movies and shouting above the radio. Even in smaller communities the automobile has tended to isolate the individual by taking him from communion with those who could have afforded him the intimacy bred of repeated association. Boys court girls across the town or in the next town as easily as down the block. As John Dewey pointed out in *The Public and Its Problems:*

> Evils which are uncritically and indiscriminately laid at the door of industrialism and democracy might, with greater intelligence, be referred to the dislocation and unsettlement of local communities. Vital and thorough attachments are bred only in the intimacy of an intercourse which is of necessity restricted in range.

It is difficult to appreciate that this is revolution; that it affects the organization of our lives and what we can give to and get from our relationships with others.

By remaining blind, by clinging to our old emotional values, we cannot stop the progress of events; we shall merely be submerged by them. A man can't make a living selling flags after parades have passed, nor a woman dress her children in swaddling clothes and keep them little. By acknowledging the changing situation and understanding it and our own reactions to it, we can act more effectively and in the end preserve some of the old precious values. We need not have a change in our method of government, we need not abandon the basic principles of our democracy, *if* we recognize the revolutionary changes which have already occurred and are continually occurring. It is only if, in our fear of drastic change, of violent change, we shut our eyes and avoid recognition of what is, that violence will surely follow. The document of revolution need not be signed and sealed in blood and horror if we have faith in ourselves and our ends and, strong in that faith, accept the fact of revolutionary transition.

Consciously, we do not recognize that this modern revolution affects us. The wars have touched our seas and skies and earth, our trade, our rhetoric, our gas, our sugar and our taxes, it is true; but we are scarcely touched by an understanding that these wars are symptoms of a revolutionary movement as profound as that which gave the world the double feature of 1775 and 1789. The American Revolutionary War and the wars of revolutionary France were not themselves revolutions but expressions of the revolutions that were going on. Like earthquakes, they were the violent and visible expression of readjustments previously unnoticed.

Nevertheless, in our unconscious we have no such ignorance. We know that runaway fortunes of bankers and speculators are in twilight, and that great concentrations of property will be skimmed by taxes. We know, too, that irresponsible competition for private satisfaction will not again be what it was when the shoots of young enterprise struggled to survive and became the giant boles of American industry. We are beginning to realize that people whom we have held in vassalage or contempt, or both, are declaring their maturity, are defying the rules of western European and American empire that the white man must be the winner.

Our allegiances to old slogans are becoming uncertain and faltering, and our confidence in our historic institutions is often jittery. We cry out "Democracy" as we might be calling "Mother" in ecstasy or despair; or we warn of "Dictatorship" as we might in terror or hatred shout "Villain." The concepts are no longer clear. We swear by the principles of representative government and swear at the faltering tedium of congressional and parliamentary delay. We want our civil rights, but we fear the effects of extending them to others. We look to the federal government in Washington for aid and support, but we resent its indifference to our local needs and habits. We want wise men to govern us but without power—doctors who know the cures but will not operate. We want to know things, and we want our children to learn—that is, know and learn anything except the things we fear.

The results upon our national life are conflicting, irritating, enervating. We have not yet to any great extent given outlet to these inner conflicts by the sadism or the hopelessness of totalitarian purges and the brutal competition of fascist nations, nor have we yet found release in the compulsive blood-lust of war. We have to a large degree suppressed recognition of the conflicting drives in our social and economic life and recognition of the facts of a revolutionary world. We have hidden them behind brave words of the Victorian age—such words as democratic, liberal, order, competition, freedom, sacred contract—many of them changed in meaning or dated by the whole trend of economic and social life. We have a sentimental nostalgia for these old concepts. They are like a house we love revisited—if we use it year after year, we do not see the changes in it or in ourselves. Only absence or the most courageous effort will make us see the change in the place and in our relationship to it. We cling, too, to the words of our youth and their early connotations as though this gave us a signal with which, if we wished, we could recall a past in which our elders could assume responsibilities for us and make wrong things right.

It is important to remember also that, although the seeds of competitive capitalism were present in medieval times, church and state and guild rather effectively controlled industry. Men did their business to live, not to create profits and wealth. Society was organized to achieve satisfactions on a more spiritual and personal basis. Competitive capitalism, itself the child of recent revolution, made new possibilities of wealth greatly exceeding the limited possibilities of wealth in land; and this gave rise to new symbols of satisfaction. The present revolutionary era arises out of the failure of those symbols, and out of the failure of wealth and competition and contractual inequality to give us satisfaction.

One of the most important symbols of the last two centuries has been the symbol of success—success in terms of dollars-and-cents rewards. This, as Margaret Mead has pointed out, has been accompanied by "a moral attitude towards life, a belief that success is the result of effort, the reward for saving, self-denial, and hard work, and a dependence upon the self for one's fate in the world." This belief is combined with elements of fear and guilt. "As success is the reward of virtue it is also the proof of virtue; to fail is to be branded as having sinned." But as these are elements in the world far beyond the control of the middle class man, swept by the hurricanes of war, competition and technical development, "his success has never lain fully in his own hands as his creed has taught him to believe. This discrepancy between the belief that virtue is always rewarded by upward social mobility and the fact that it often is not, is a continual breeding ground for fear and insecurity."

Out of fear and insecurity and guilt comes a whole cycle of destructive forces. Men rebel against ideas which have failed them. They seek to destroy those institutions which haunt them with the guilty fear of failure.

Another reason for our apparent inability to appreciate the revolutionary character of our age is Marxian propaganda, which regards only a "class" revolution and the destruction of the bourgeoisie by the proletariat as in effect a genuine revolution. By this test one must wait until the conclusion of an era to determine *ex post facto* whether it was revolutionary. To the Marxian, even the affairs led by Mussolini in Italy and Hitler in Germany were no revolutions.

So, too, the propaganda of fascism plays ducks and drakes with the word "revolution." That propaganda which was accepted during the decade of the thirties by many Americans and by the most influential people in Britain, declared that fascism was no revolution but a mere speed-up of efficiency, a veritable bulwark of the capitalist system, a barrier against communism. It was common to hear that Mussolini made the Italian trains run on time and abolished brigandage; and "that's not revolution." This decoy deceived millions of people as to the revolutionary nature of fascism.

What has brought about this revolutionary situation? It is too glib a solution to offer the Marxian answer of dialectical materialism, to suggest that economic causes are the sole causes. The search for the ethical and psychological values, the ethical and psychological motivations of men—which are not alone economic—offer a better hypothesis of the primary cause. It is no more correct to say that the decadence of capitalism brought about this condition of revolution than to say that a wife runs away from home because of a dispute with her husband over her pin-money. The dispute may exist. There may be a disagreement as to pin-money, but this is not really the cause of the separation; rather, it is, the particular one of a number of situations on which their emotional conflict fixes.

Although the decline of capitalist economy is not the basic or only cause of the twentieth-century revolution, it does play a part in the world's crisis; and therefore it must be studied. It is one of the disappointments and weaknesses, which is not overlooked and forgiven, on which emotional conflicts are fixed among groups of people and among nations. In such a study, not only the ethical and psychological values of capitalism must be considered, but also its relation to its contemporaries, liberalism and the parliamentary state.

The nineteenth-century state, continuing into the twentieth century, which defended property and contract rights and granted aids and benefits, was devoid of power to plan or co-ordinate. Competition was left to its own fratricidal tendencies, and the power to distribute lagged more and more behind the capacity to produce. The struggle for markets and raw materials made cannibals of the successful, left insolvent bones by the wayside and finally took the red corpuscles out of the competitive system. What is left is essentially a group of cartels and monopolies, cumbersome brontosauruses ready to devour democratic principles and democratic mechanics in self-defense, as they have in their fields already chewed up free competition.

How these modern monsters failed to adjust themselves to crisis is described in that almanac of the wealthy, *Fortune* magazine for May, 1942:

> A modern industrial plant is an enormous aggregation of capital, labor and other vested interests; so many livelihoods are involved in it that it does not dare entrust itself to the caprices of a wholly free market. . . . And competition, which always did tend to issue in somebody's victory, produced industrial mammoths whose prices were administered and whose power rivaled that of many a state.
>
> When the depression brought an end to Wall Street's last great merger era, the American economy therefore proved even more inflexible and constipated than the British. Our mammoths could not afford to deflate, so we got unemployment instead.

The parliamentary state, the child of capitalist economy, was regarded with greater merit when it least interfered with the competitive system. This is the meaning of the adage, "That state governs best which governs least." The rights of private property and private contract were "sacred" rights—they were called "natural" rights, which meant that their origin, like Nature in general, was Divine and could not be interfered with by monarchs or by parliaments. Business enterprises, those independent youngsters, required an arena for their growth and development. This they could never have attained under the paternalistic hand of the seventeenth- and eighteenth-century state, which distributed monopolies to favorites—the tea trade of India, the gold of Mexico, the farmlands of Virginia, or the furs of Canada. In their struggle they wanted Father to be quiescent, to stand on the sidelines and cheer as he watched their muscles swell.

Edmund Burke, who was an eloquent spokesman for the new order of the industrial revolution, believed that in the political field "the monopoly of authority is, in every instance and in every degree, an evil"; but held that "the monopoly of capital is the contrary." The laws of commerce were to him the laws of Nature "and consequently the laws of God." Neither the government as government nor the rich as rich ought "to supply to the poor those necessaries which it has pleased the Divine Providence for a while to withhold from them." To him it was only the malignity, perverseness and ill-governed passions of mankind, particularly envy for one another's property, that prevented men from seeing and acknowledging with thankfulness to the benign Dispenser that the farmer was entitled to the "full incoming profit on the product of his labour." It is, in fact, this divine Dispenser who "obliges men, whether they will or not, in pursuing their own selfish interests, to connect the general good with their own individual success." He might more properly have said that the individually successful identified his own success with the general good, and in this way his guilt for causing young children to work in mines for twelve or fourteen hours a day was cleansed by the knowledge that it was for the general good—and any uneasy conscience which might be stirred by pursuing one's own selfish interest could be quieted by the pious conviction that God had ordained it as "enlightened self-interest."

Diderot held that the possessor of property was its absolute master. He and he alone had the power of kings over it to use or to abuse it. Government had no right, he believed, to deal with the abuses or uses of property; for if it did, then there would be "an end to any true notion of property or liberty."

Ricardo, expressing the classic economic notion of the nineteenth century, held that private property in land and capital must at all times be protected and free contracts between individuals enforced. Property and contract were sacred; they were to be respected above individuals.

Now, lest anyone think that Burke and Diderot and Ricardo expressed merely the current ideas of the eighteenth- and nineteenth-century braintrusters, and that the man of affairs had no such ideas, I would refer him to the mine strike in the United States in 1902. At that time one George F. Baer, president of a Pennsylvania mine company, stated the case in this language:

> The rights and interests of the laboring man will be protected and cared for—not by the labor agitators, but by the Christian men to whom God in His infinite wisdom has given the control of the property interests of this country.

Furthermore, when these men chosen of God—in this case, one suspects Mammon to be the divine spirit in question—have found that the sacredness of their rights has not been respected, they have not hesitated to risk the welfare of their country in the preservation and support of their mandate from the gods. Thus, during the struggle to continue the Second National Bank in the United States, Biddle, the leading American banker of his day, deliberately caused financial stringency in the country. Time and again liberal movements in France were checked by the manipulations of the discount rate by the Banque de France. Company guards and state police shot workers who questioned the "Christian" conduct of the "Christian" men to whom God had given the control of property interests.

At this point it is well to give warning that we must be careful not to infuse into a discussion of capitalism the emotional attachment to the old school team. It is not the school team, to be cheered no matter by how much it is losing; nor is it the rival team to be hooted regardless of how well it performs. Some of us want to cling to the concepts of capitalism and capitalistic competition because they are old familiars and homey; others among us grudge them the slightest praise or concession of vitality because they have disappointed us, and we prefer the greater destruction of class competition. In all accuracy, capitalism has proved to be a useful engine developing more productive power than any previous engine; but for years before this present war the competitive system had to be insulated against international competition through tariffs and manipulations of currency and metallic standards and through armed intervention to gain control of raw materials; and capital invested at home had to be supported by grants in aid to build railroads and ships and homes, to open up new resources and to establish banking and credit facilities.

This means that the old boiler has been replaced by an electric motor. New parts have been substituted, and they do not always fit the old machine. It may have to be rebuilt considerably more if it is to work, and then it will no longer be the old Adam Smith steam engine. State planning will never leave capitalism the same broad sweep of freedom that it had; and this regardless of whether the eventual outcome will be the strait-jacketing prescribed by the neurotic doctors of fascism or a more moderate control by democratic methods. State planning is here to be with us a long time because unplanned private finance milked new capital investment, and because industry could not plan either for world markets or internally. To some extent this was so, as in the United States, because some people took the competitive system at its word and, through anti-trust acts, prohibited industrial planning.

Let us remember, then, that capitalism and the competitive system, and the parliamentary state too, are mechanisms which men have created for mankind; and, like all machinery, they must be judged by their effectiveness rather than by passionate loyalty, fear or hatred. In *Erewhon*, Samuel Butler abolishes machinery and relegates it to the museum. In the play *Dynamo* the hero falls in love with an electric generator. This is the stuff of fiction; but social problems are not solved by a resort to fictions; they are merely reduced to angry orgies of emotion.

Capitalism in its various phases has certainly served a useful purpose. In the modern era the state monopolies granted in the mercantile period made possible, in areas such as the Americas and India, the development of sources of raw material which were a first step in the abolition of want and periodic starvation. The period of industrial capitalism and private initiative created the factory system, which replaced slow and laborious hand production with the possibilities of multiplying goods so that vastly more people could obtain the benefits of more and better clothing, food and housing. At the same time it created a labor supply which made that greater production possible.

Industrialism arose on the foundations of mercantilism; it depended upon ample supplies of raw products and a more fluid labor supply for the increased production of consumer goods. The finance-capitalist phase, in which the banker succeeded the adventurer—that is, the captain of the expedition—and in which the industrialist succeeded the captain of industry as the dynamo of the economic system, made possible such mobilization of capital and concentration of industrial control as gave to the world the production line. And it is the production line which has made it possible to produce consumer goods enough for the entire population of the world. From good, cheap, stylish dresses to good, cheap cars and good, cheap preserved foods, industry could, if it would, give to every family the means of comfortable living and the certainty that the supply will not be a matter of the day only.

These are genuine gains for the people of the world. There is assurance in the very knowledge that such a potentiality exists. It is as beneficial and reassuring as the knowledge that medical science can cure many diseases and prevent much suffering and that sanitation can avoid plague and discomfort.

But for all its contributions, capitalism has shown, in increasing ratio, serious defects. Either it must control markets and thus limit the amount of production as a cushion against accumulating surpluses on which it would have to take a loss; or its units must compete with each other and thus squeeze the profits out of the enterprise. It is in a further quandary in that it must pay sufficient wages to assure the purchasing power to buy its products; but if it makes this assurance possible, the cost must eventually exceed the public purse.

In conflict with the need to create increased purchasing power is the technical development of industry which replaces man-power by machine operations and remote electrical control. Capitalism has therefore competed for new markets and tended in essential industries to monopolize the older ones. It has, where it could, driven out small producers. It has alternately expanded (inflated) and contracted (deflated). It has given work and produced unemployment, improved technical productive capacity and suppressed new technical inventions which, though they might multiply consumer goods, would also destroy the value of present plant.

Now, do not for a moment suppose that these fluctuations are planned or that they are even foreseen by the majority of producers. They are like a holiday crowd. When the weather is fair they jam the beaches; when it is wet they stay at home.

Capitalism as it has developed, like other institutions and like individuals, has tended to rationalize its activities; but its own insecurity has caused it to abandon the idea of the sacredness and inviolability of private property. Its advocates speak of it as essential to efficient production but no longer as part of a "Divine plan." It has served a valuable use in the modern world; but, like the steel-pointed, horse-drawn plow which replaced the pointed stick, or the spinning wheel which replaced the spindle, it has proved inadequate to provide security and to fulfill the consumer needs of the world.

A fundamentalist view of private property is, then, hardly in order today. Man will no longer believe in the sacredness of property or the miracles that private ownership can perform. Capital is no longer untouchable except by the initiate. Its control is no longer a matter solely for the priesthood of Wall Street, the City of London, and the Bourses of Paris, Amsterdam and Berlin. (The stockholder's vote has long since been reduced to a rubber stamp in big industry.) In recent decades the state and labor organizations have interfered more and more with the techniques of profit making.

But, though a fundamentalist view of property is untenable today, it does not follow that private property must be abolished or that state capitalism must be substituted for private capitalism. God is not destroyed because the Bible is not literally interpreted—because, for example, men do not believe that the creation occurred in six days. The great monopolies of the mercantile era did not wipe out merchant trading on an international scale. The factory system left a field for the handicrafts. Henry Ford and many small industries have found capital without recourse to the investment banker and continued to control their own businesses. Even under state planning, individual initiative can have opportunities. Only the hand of state capitalism can destroy such initiative. In other words, it is a fallacy to say that what has failed to fulfill men's needs can be discarded like an old car. It is also false to argue that there is no alternative.

While it would hardly be true to say that social progress can be only by revolution, it is certainly true that the death struggles of reactionaries have not brought progress. They cannot create but only concede, for their hearts are in the past and their fears in all the future, so that instead of guiding and modifying the trends of revolution, they are destroyed by the mobility of the institutions which in their fears they have set up as bulwarks to all eternity. We must proceed, then, on the theory that there is no perpetuity to our institutions and seek the basis of those institutions in the aims and behavior of men.

How much of private capitalism will remain in a world in which free contract will be circumscribed and governments will be major participants in economic planning, it is impossible to know. How much we are endangered by the threat of state capitalism is also uncertain. But it seems that, though the objectives of individual enterprise will be altered and the experience of individual enterprise get new values, it need not and should not be dead when the war ends. Surely competition and totalitarianism are not the only alternatives. The emphasis of free enterprise may be transmuted from the individualistic expression of capitalism to a co-operative free enterprise—to a collaboration of equals rather than to a dictatorship, however beneficent. For in large part this is a war of people against states—it is a revolution by men who for the first time are conscious in masses that they are attaining maturity. It is their revolution against paternalism in many forms.

The common people of the world—the workers in America and Great Britain, the farmers in Russia, the coolies in China, the mystery-ridden crowds of India, yes, and the disillusioned people of Italy and the fantasy-inspired youth of Germany and Japan—are in rebellion against the pattern of being held down by some person or group, by some other race or nation. They do not want to be told that they are not good enough or not capable enough or not developed enough to be treated as equals. The world-wide revolution of our generation is essentially democratic in that it is, for all its quirks and vagaries, a war against paternalism.

2

Liberty, Equality and Fraternity

THE WORLD OF INDUSTRY, commerce and democratic government of the nineteenth and twentieth centuries, in western Europe and America expressed itself in the political and economic philosophy of liberalism. The heart of liberalism has been individual initiative; competition has been its pulse and Liberty its battle credo. Neither equality nor fraternity, however, could find more than a verbal place in its system; for equality would have required a state which redressed the balance between weak and strong; and for fraternity to be realized it was essential that there be a minimum of competition, a diet on which the economic order of capitalism and international mercantilism could not survive.

The utilitarian adage that society is organized to secure the greatest good for the greatest number pulled the punch of the equalitarian slogans of the American and French Revolutions. "Liberty and Justice for all"—"the Brotherhood of man under the Fatherhood of God"—here was the stuff of oratory, the bell button to set off the applause of electrified audiences. But did not Liberty too often degenerate into license? Men, of course, were not really born equal. Fraternity was a noble ideal and, like the Sermon on the Mount, could be well pondered in church on a Sunday morning.

It was rather the resonant ethical note of the utilitarians that lifted the nineteenth- and early twentieth-century spirit, brought balm to the starched-collar conscience and embalmed the thinking processes of generations who throve and, in general, lived in peace during the era of industrial development, the period of what is sometimes called the *Pax Britannica*.

In theory, Liberty and Equality were extended to every class in society, to every creed and color—that is, liberty to compete, equality of right to compete, if one had the chance to do so. One hundred and fifty years ago, even one hundred years ago, before ownership was broadcast, while industry was owned and operated by the same man, while the work of the hand was not so completely divorced from the machine as it is today, the inequalities were not so grave but that hundreds of thousands could compete and get a run for their money. Even now there have been exceptions enough who have been able to compete successfully and thus prove the rule.

Of course, Fraternity was something else, for after all there were "niggers" and the "heathen Chinee." Fraternity might be all right for men like Robespierre, who could guillotine everyone he did not want as a brother or sister, but that was impractical. So fraternity was not taken too seriously.

This is not to say that the people whose interests were

dominant in the political philosophy and practices of the nineteenth century did not make concessions to liberty and equality and to those groups of the population who felt, even though they could not articulate that feeling, that those terms meant something more than free competition. So, as capital wealth multiplied, its possessors could afford to yield greater powers of political expression to the propertyless; and thus gradually in western Europe and the United States manhood suffrage and eventually woman suffrage became the rule. (While Father holds the purse strings he can afford to let the children talk; and the greater the purse the more freedom he can allow them without forfeiting his power or feeling that he has lost anything of his old virility.) In those lands, however, which were not greatly mechanized and which were still semi-feudal, the extension of suffrage offered no returns to those with power and found no population sufficiently enlightened and possessed of enough counter-power to press the point.

The extension of suffrage afforded a justification for the doctrine of a society aimed to achieve the greatest good for the greatest number, because in this way there was established an officially recognized greater number who could give explicit endorsement at the polls to the greater good. The greater good, obviously, was free competition—stimulated by grants in aid, it is true—and of the mythical *status quo*. This new electorate, this greater number of whom the utilitarians spoke, could choose between high and low tariffs and between public servants; but it dared not question the uses to which private property was put or the sanctity of private contracts. No person in responsible position would suggest any doubt as to the equality of bargaining power between employer and worker, for that was a vital incident to free contract.

In other words, the children were growing up and so they could order their own dinner. Only, Father still decided the rules of the game, whether the order was to be *table d'hôte* or *à la carte*. Bad boys and girls might question Father's authority to make decisions and insist on ordering *à la carte* when he had said *table d'hôte*. But Father had ways of retaliating—he called it punishment. It was only bad citizens, dangerous agitators, religious fanatics who inquired who it was gave the right to determine what was the greatest good, what the greatest number, and who was to do the appraising and counting. There were means short of the guillotine for dealing with such people: prison, loss of job, the blacklist or social ostracism.

Thus it is plain that equality was circumscribed by rugged individualism; it was stalled and quartered by competitive inequality. The doughnuts were in the center of the table where all might come and get them—the timid soul, the paralytic and the man with the boardinghouse reach—and who do you think got most?

What we are participating in today is not just an ideological realignment, not a mere breakdown in the economic machine worn by the friction of competition. Men are coming of age, and all the revolutionary drives of adolescense are coming into prominence. The conscience of man is confused; it is disturbed to the point of anger because liberty has not proven to be liberty; equality has not given equality; fraternity has been ignored. Words, words—and men want satisfaction of their needs.

The very fact that technical development on farm and in factory has shown them the possibility of achieving a world of plenty has stimulated them all the more to desire plenty and to seek the satisfaction of that desire.

> If the technological age can provide mankind with a firm and general basis of material security, it will be absorbed in a humane age [John Dewey writes in *The Public and Its Problems*]. But without passage through a machine age, mankind's hold upon what is needful as a precondition of a free, flexible and many-colored life is so precarious and inequitable that competitive scramble for acquisition and frenzied use of the results of acquisition for purposes of excitation and display will be perpetuated.

The machine age can indeed bring greater security to life and more opportunity for a "free, flexible and many-colored life." It can make hunger and rags and hovels bad dreams of other nights; but even the broad distribution of economic security cannot be relied on to exterminate the competitive scramble of the drive to acquire more of something than some other fellow has or avoid the misuse of what one does possess. There will still be the frenzied lust for power to compensate for real or imagined inadequacies.

The problem is more than one of plenty, more than improving the means of distribution and guaranteeing economic security. To be certain of food and shelter tomorrow and next month and next year is important to enable men to release energies otherwise entangled with the fear of hunger and the elements; but that certainty will not assure satisfactory use of those energies. It will not of itself make obsolete all those thousands upon thousands of things that men and women do to obtain self-assurance, to prove to themselves that they are not inadequate. Variety will continue, and with it a sense of inequality and defeat and often guilt. Nor will these psychological by-products of variation be removed by numerical equality of wealth or income or by state ownership of the means of production so long as people confuse equivalence with identity.

In childhood we ask identical treatment with other members of the family—with our brothers and sisters, with our mother and father. It is not enough to be told that when we are bigger we shall be permitted to stay up later in the evening or shall receive an allowance of a dime a week; nor is it sufficient to be told that when we were younger mother used to do our buttons and prepare something special for us to eat as she does for the baby. Our sense of being ourselves is still uncertain. From time to time we want to be in fact father or mother, brother or sister. We want the advantages that accrue to each relationship, to each sex, to each age. Out of this infantile confusion, out of this urge to realize ourselves through identification with other persons, comes our later confusion of equality with identity. Just as we identified ourselves as infants with the other members of our home in order to justify gaining for ourselves what was due to them because of their needs, so in later years we tend to ask for identical treatment although we know perfectly well our needs may be different and that we ourselves cannot render identical treatment, but only equivalent treatment, to others. In all women there is a touch of the extreme feminist who wants to go all places that men go and do all things that men do regardless of differences in physical capacity. To the extent that they are unwilling to accept their femininity they will feel frustrated. When there is a shortage of gasoline and it is rationed many of us feel aggrieved if we do not receive the maximum allotment, though we know that our need for motoring is not the same as that of the man who must use his car to get to work in the airplane factory or that of the country doctor who must drive to his patients.

Even after we know that our capacities and facilities are different from those of the other members of the family, the old pattern disturbs us and sets up conflicts behind the façade of our conscious thought. Thus young people frequently choose an occupation for which they may not be well fitted just because a brother or a friend is doing the same thing. Then they are dissatisfied and feel aggrieved that more or better work is expected of them. They become the clock-watchers of industry and the professions.

We often begrudge others a recognition of their achievements or their different needs; we take those achievements and differences as discrimination or a threat against us. We may acknowledge that someone else has more skill and training than we, but nevertheless resent greater rewards or applause going to him, because we see in it a form of discrimination. Why should he get a higher mark at school or a better salary or a prettier girl or more praise? It is the pattern we knew as infants when our parents rewarded our brother for something he had done, something we had not done—and that had not seemed right, equitable.

Frequently, too, we identify ourselves with someone, or some group, which we have invested with heroic features. Then criticism or failure of such a person, or group, becomes again a threat to us; their successes are our successes. Such identification may take place with a parent, a dictator, a baseball player, an actress, a minister, a political party, a religious sect, a business venture—any number of persons or associations. There is no one of us who has not had such an experience and cannot think of illustrations. When a Jewish businessman is criticized for some act of his, Jews are likely to take it as an attack on them and call the criticism anti-Semitism. When a Catholic bishop is criticized for opposing birth-control legislation, Catholics tend to regard this as an attack on their religion—it is anti-Catholic. When the newspapers describe the alleged pickpocket as colored, the Negroes may protest that this is an attempt to besmirch all Negroes and is race discrimination.

In 1908, when Fred Merkel failed to touch second base in the deciding baseball game between the New York Giants and the Chicago Cubs, there was not a boy in New York who did not identify with Merkel and feel cheated, angry and chagrined; nor was there a boy in Chicago who did not feel identity with Johnny Evers and a sense of elation at the way he had out-smarted Merkel. Read Hull for Merkel, America for Giants, man and woman for boy, Tojo for Evers, Japanese for Chicago, and December 7, 1941, for 1908, and you have the same pattern of emotions.

The chief business of adolescence is to emerge from the half-born state of infancy and to realize ourselves as individuals, to recognize the fact that variations exist and how we differ from others. As we grow up we identify farther afield from the family group and gradually live more and more as ourselves and less as the self-masked impersonators of others. This process of growth gives rise to those moods of antagonism toward parents and teachers, who seem to be denying recognition of emerging individuality and variety, alternating with moods of passionate attachment to family and school or some particular person. Here the child is seeking to be acknowledged, now as a big shot, as the stuff that heroes and moving-picture stars are made of, tomorrow as an infant to be protected and cuddled, as an infant is protected and cuddled. The need for rewards and punishments is less immediate than in infancy. Rewards and punishments can be related to our action though administered less directly and deferred.

The patterns of adolescence, like the patterns of infancy, are not entirely escaped in maturity, but leave their imprints on all of us, their scars on most of us. We achieve maturity to the degree that we realize ourselves as individuals, accepting the fact that there are a multitude of differences between us and our family, our friends and others—differences of physical and mental capacity, facility, experience, background and needs to be satisfied. To achieve maturity we must also learn to share with others and to act with others without the fear that thereby we are losing out; we must learn that we cannot hurt without either losing caste in our own eyes or being hurt in retribution; and, nevertheless, that there are times in which one must act to the harm of others in self-defense, without extraneous anger. The police may stop a barroom brawl or a man resist burglars or the Greeks defend their lands against Mussolini's army without a sense of guilt because irresponsible and sadistic actions cannot be stopped by closing one's eyes to them forever. Destructive hysteria, like any hysteria, can only be treated with dispassionate firmness.

One of the important factors in the maturing process, then, is the development of an appreciation of the distinction between identity and equivalence and the acceptance of differences without a sense of being cheated. This is an important concept, because it is essential to humanizing abstractions such as liberty and equality. In terms of behavior, liberty and equality represent the liberation of spiritually and emotionally grown men and women from infantile limitations which at an earlier stage prevented them from achieving the development of their individual selves free of the need for identification. At a later stage in development, liberty and equality also represent liberation from adolescent frustrations which were inherent in the personal uncertainty of boys and girls as to the extent of their dependence upon and independence of the family group. To spiritually and emotionally grown men and women, liberty and equality represent, in terms of behavior, not just an urge to achieve a level of uniformity, not just the submergence of self in a mass of equivalent units, but rather the mutual acceptance of the right of each person to his own form of variation and to his own form of personal development.

The principles of maturity apply not only to the maturing process of men themselves, but also to their institutions. As religion developed from primitive idolatry, demon worship and taboo into the great ethical faiths of the East and the West, it emphasized the equality of men before God and gave testimony to the inestimable worth of all men irrespective of the variety of their origins and personal attributes. We need not now discuss the paternalistic stream in religious belief and practice which has often held men back from a realization of this equality; for our purposes it is sufficient to note that it has been not the paternalistic feature, but the equalitarian, which has been the stimulating element.

The basic principle of equality in Judeo-Christian doctrine, however, could not be brought to earth because there was no mechanism by which church and state could be compelled to administer with equity or to the disadvantage of power. The medieval state and church, with exceptions, relied upon the goodness of the individual man to do equity. In practice this generally meant the goodness of the anointed man, the man with power. The lesser men of the Middle Ages were not trusted; they were tainted by original sin; and, free of paternalistic superintendence, they might be expected to go and sin again. But once more the dynamic force in modern political institutions has been the achievement by the lesser man of self-confidence and a degree of freedom from paternalism. This has made possible a limitation of that arbitrary power which could disregard the worth of the individual man.

The retrogression to a renewed disregard of human individuality and personal worth is the greatest threat of the totalitarian philosophy to democratic peoples. That is why such a philosophy is incompatible with religions based on ethical principles of equity and freedom for individual spiritual development. That is why it is incompatible with an organization of society aimed to achieve equitable treatment of each member.

The struggle between the democratic and the totalitarian

approach to life, the clash between the attitudes of these two ideologies toward individual man, is an old conflict, old in its pattern in the history of the race, old, too, in the emotional conflicts in each one of us. Men have sought on the one hand what they have called justice or equity, and on the other domination or power. Here is the background of human society, the struggle between power and equity, between privilege and equality. The protagonists are eternally elders and brothers, fathers and sons. (It should be needless to say that no sex distinction is intended.) In early times it was the elders, the wizards, the medicine men of the tribe who formed themselves into secret semi-religious or clan societies to protect established custom, to enforce totem and taboo, to conserve tradition. They invoked the name, the blessing or the spirit of the ancestral ghost, or the totem animal, or the aid of some magic instrument. The past and the supernatural were their allies in resisting innovation, in preserving their power over the younger men. From earliest times, too, the sons struggled for equality among themselves—the organization of society was such that combat with the elders which might result in their murder was more appalling in its dangers than such an act would be even today. The brothers, though they might not dare to risk their father Jacob's curse by killing him or Joseph, had to put Joseph out of the way, for his coat of many colors was a sign of favoritism that threatened their security in the patriarchal clan.

In this early society of the clan or *gens*, except for the privileges of the patriarch—that is, the head of the family —and the special rights, which also involved special risks, of the medicine man, equality was the rule. Members of the group had little personal property they could call their own; they were assured of what food and shelter and covering for their bodies the clan possessed; they knew that their *gens* would protect them and avenge any harm done to them by outsiders. Slavery apparently was a late development arising at about the same stage of social organization in which private property in land was accepted. Inheritance was in the *gens*, although restrictions appeared in the case of daughters marrying out of the *gens*.

Lewis H. Morgan wrote in *Ancient Society:*

> During the Later Period of barbarism a new element, that of aristocracy, had a marked development. The individuality of persons, and the increase of wealth now possessed by individuals in masses, were laying the foundation of personal influence. Slavery, also, by permanently degrading a portion of the people, tended to establish contrasts of conditions unknown in the previous ethnical periods. This, with property and official position, gradually developed the sentiment of aristocracy which has so deeply penetrated modern society, and antagonized the democratical principles created and fostered by the gentes. It soon disturbed the balance of society by introducing unequal privileges, and degrees of respect for individuals among people of the same nationality, and thus became the source of discord and strife.

With the increase in wealth new powers come into the hands of the head men. To those physical weapons and those psychological instruments of tradition and magic which the elders had possessed, were now added economic weapons. Thus indeed the balance of society was disturbed; freedom became more limited and inequality entrenched.

This is not to say, as Rousseau did, that the happy savage was a free man enjoying natural rights. The men of barbarian ages were not free men. They were the bondmen of real and fanciful fears of the same basic design as are men today. But the methods of social pressure were different, and there was less distinction between man and man. An attempt to attain power uninvited was always a threat to the security of those persons who were there first—the father, the patriarch, the elder, the medicine man—and thus stimulated them to vengeance against the presumptuous ones. Equality was just, and therefore he who sought special privilege or power was doing wrong in the eyes of his fellows, for he was threatening their portion.

The growth of wealth and the power of property, as we have seen, destroyed the balance of brotherhood, the community nature of the means of subsistence. The distortion of equal treatment, although it appeared in many forms, was symbolized by the law of primogeniture, the law that gave all to the oldest son. It was more than this law, it was all that lay behind this symbolism, all that humiliated the dignity of the common man, that made Gerrard Winstanley, the "Digger" pamphleteer, cry out in 1652:

> Others say, "It is true *Freedom*, that the elder Brother shall be Landlord of the Earth, and the younger Brother a Servant: And this is but half Freedom, and begets murmurings, wars, and quarrels."

There are thus two angles to the achievement of equality: one the drive to fraternal sharing, the other the drive to escape parental dominion. These are psychological drives in the struggle for equality. If we grow normally, there comes a time when we feel we should no longer bear the yoke of our youth. We witness daily the crippling effect upon children—an effect which persists all their lives—where parents refuse to surrender domination over the lives of their children. We see, too, the beneficial effects upon young people of independence gradually realized. They may do things that appear to be crazy, to be vulgar, to be different from those that the older generation did when it was young; but if parents and teachers accept the facts of variety without a sense of frustration, there need be little friction between generations. When parents and teachers can treat their young people with respect, as contemporaries, then one can expect a healthy development of maturity.

If, however, the elders attempt to suppress the young, if they make young people feel that they are wrong or sinful to depart from the ways of their fathers—in other words, if older people cannot accept as anything but a threat to themselves the variations of young people as to capacity, interests or behavior from standards set by the older people —then conflict does indeed arise, though it may in large part be repressed. The reaction of the young man and woman may be open rebellion, surly hatred or lassitude. It depends upon whether they are the run-away type, the sadistic or the "yes ma-ma." Bondage, continual paternalism do not make a mature people. They make a frightened, a subservient, a sullen or a bloodlusting people.

Those same humane, protective traits which cause people to make sacrifices for their young unfortunately also persist through the adolescence of the children and make it difficult for elders to yield liberty to children. The little child gives the parent a sense of strength and wisdom. There is security in the very disparity between the strength and wisdom of the child and his parents, which it is difficult later to forego. Then, too, there is the accompanying satisfaction of creation and of sharing. It is only the rare parent, therefore, at least in highly civilized communities, who can accept with equanimity the equality of his grown children; so that if the young people want maturity enough they must cut the cord themselves. They must in one way or another declare their independence and so far as possible set out on their own road.

The independence achieved in late adolescence can usually be achieved with less scarring and bitterness on the part of the young than on that of their elders, who feel themselves so often shorn of authority and capacity. It is as though they saw an army of Lilliputians, children in serried ranks rebelling against their rightful officers and ranged against them.

This struggle for recognition as an adult, as an equal, is the life story of every normal individual. It is also the life story of every class in society which has escaped from slavery, serfdom or some form of domination or control by groups better established in power. As it achieves a sense of growing strength, of greater competency and understanding, each social and racial and economic group demands that it be treated as adult—insists on being regarded as contemporary, as a people with present, not as a stagnant agglomeration, not as a people who will some day in the future be worthy of handling their own affairs.

Liberty, Equality and Fraternity

This is what the democratic revolution going on in the world today means. It is at times vague and disorganized and adolescent. At moments it is an attempt to throw off all restraints, and then a dash for the rewards and protection of a father-figure.

I have spent so much space in considering the psychological patterns of childhood because they reach not only into the lives of adults as individuals, but also into their group lives. People do not cease to be the same people, or escape their own emotional texture, by becoming political beings or by working at a means of livelihood. When they seek liberty they are moved or obsessed by the same emotional designs that prompt the adolescent to escape from familiar paternalism. When they ask equality, they often ask for identical treatment, as they did when they were little children; but more often they are only asking to be treated as grownups, capable of developing their own salvation. If they have not the right of suffrage, they seek to vote. If they have not the means of procuring education for their children, medical care when they are ill, work when the boss fires them or the means of support in their old age, they move for equalizing factors which will make provision for them in these circumstances. When as individuals they are subject to the whims and prejudices of their employer, they get equality through joining together and bargaining collectively. When the industries on which their livelihood depends are not successful, they ask for a share in the responsibiliy of management. When they are subject or exploited nations, there comes a time when they demand independence and the abandonment of extra-territorial rights.

Adult men do not want to be told, "Do as you're directed,"—"You've got all that's good for you now,"—"I know best,"—"I'm doing this for your good." These are phrases familiar to childhood. They are also familiar as justifications of paternalism in industrial and political life. Men and women who have not had an arrested adolescence resent such talk. When they have the means to do so, they rebel against such attitudes; they seek to free themselves from benevolent as well as malign dictators; they attempt to raise themselves to a level of equality so that their governments and their employers will talk to them man to man. It is this recognition by the common man of his maturity that is at the basis of our twentieth-century revolution. For the battle array is the common man emerging from adolescence against those who would retain a paternalistic control.

Let us look again and see why it is that parents have such difficulty acknowledging that their children no longer need them, why the man with power cannot readily let go of it. In early times for the head of the family or the clan to lose power meant quite literally his destruction. Even today loss of power leaves most people with a sense of having been somehow crippled. It is a phase of what the Freudians call the castration complex. But it is not altogether a groundless dread, this fear of losing control. For we know from studies of psychology that men and women can love and hate the same objects; and those in power recall in their own unconscious memory, if not consciously, their own murderous instincts against persons who exercised authority over their youth—even persons they loved and with whom they at times identified. The degree to which those in power can yield equality to maturing groups is the measure of their own achievement of maturity, of their capacity to understand that there is strength to be found in the communion of equals and in creative effort as well as in the power to call others to heel.

So inevitably bad blood and hatred comes between socially adolescent men and socially paternalistic men, and in the process values become distorted. Property is no longer for sustenance and pleasure; it is a weapon. Work is no more a means of self-expression and of livelihood, but for profit; and possession becomes an accumulation of reserves of power. In the fight against the elders, against paternalism, property is not a surety against want. It is again power. Loss of property is no longer an ill which may bring want and suffering; it is in itself a form of bodily injury, of mayhem, a loss of sword and staff.

Frequently the very purpose of the brothers fighting for equality is lost sight of as the individual becomes submerged in the group. In the closed ranks of the fighters there is no recognition of human variety, no hope of each man's exercising his special talents or satisfying his particular needs. We can see among revolutionaries, as among the orthodox, that those who question mass action are dissenters and dissenters are deemed to be in league with the incarnate devil whose powers are being challenged. As a result, differences become a threat to those who have joined together. If one boy tells, may they not all still be spanked? If they are to be criticized by one of their number, are they not all placed in danger? If a minority begins to enjoy dancing and cards, what is to protect the majority of Puritans from seeing the ideals for which they suffered in the wilderness lost, and levity, that child of sin and the aristocracy, destroy the Bible? If anyone could criticize the Communist party—and later Stalin—what was to prevent him from becoming strong enough to restore Czarism or challenge the control of the October Revolution?

The attempt to achieve equality, then, is hampered and confused by this spirit of group solidarity among revolutionaries, the very people who seek a new balance of equity. It is a reversion to a distinctly childhood pattern. There is no longer the satisfaction of the shared participation of equals, no enriching collaboration in an emancipation permitting each to develop in accordance with his own capacities at his own tempo. Fear and power have entered and taken control. Like the adolescent, the revolutionaries resent criticism and require praise to give them reassurance; they need to exercise their own strength to establish their sense of prestige and achievement.

Neither an individual nor a party nor a people is graduated from adolescence if he or they remain so insecure that they must guide their existence by a craving for recognition and praise, if they must forever demand rewards to attain satisfaction. Then the son becomes the immature father who must repeat the pattern of his elders as a conservator of the past in order to minister to his sense of prestige; he must demonstrate his own strength to quiet fantasies that he may suffer injury from his sons through a challenge of his authority; he must ease his sense of guilt at the fantasy that perhaps in fact he did destroy his parents.

The revolutionary government, when based on force, also repeats the pattern of its predecessors. It must conserve the past it is creating, it must wipe out all trace of ancestry to compensate its guilty fears. Thus Cromwell fighting the Stuarts and their Catholic tendencies butchered the Irish Catholics; and Robespierre, the Bourbon judge who could not condemn men to death, cut off the heads of the old regime which had cruelly immured its enemies in the Bastille; and Lenin and Trotsky and Stalin utilized the firing squad and the cold steppes of Siberia to destroy their enemies, as the Czars had done to theirs.

Perhaps the neatest case in point is the German people. For the most part, crushed between their fear of the *Verboten* and their need of praise from *Hoheit,* they must again and again exhibit their prowess to gain power and reward. For centuries the Prussians have suffered from the pressure of these infantile fears and needs. They have had to truckle to power and then dominate something. It is not accidental that the Germans have cried out for a place in the sun and for *Lebensraum.* Light and space are essential to exhibitionism. The world is not large enough for a nation in hate to reveal its strength, because in the long run even the world from which it seeks praise becomes an object of its hatred and must be destroyed. In *Mein Kampf* Hitler plays up to the British Empire; he indicates that he wishes to avoid combat with it; he wants its admiration. In the end he must try to wipe out that Empire because it is a living testimony to the German infantile weakness that asks praise even for its most atrocious deeds; and it is also living testimony to that insatiable appetite for rewards which never can prove to Hitler or his nation that they have reached maturity or are the equal of other peoples.

The greatest strength of the British has been in their comparative maturity. I say comparative because there have been cross currents of adolescence and fear which are not mature. For example, the relics of feudalism have stultified a greater realization of democracy by causing a large part of the population to defer to medieval titles, to welcome a nod or an order for truffles or cigarettes from a duke; and such relics have stimulated in thousands of Englishmen the ambition to become a baronet. Those interests which, until 1940, at least, had control in the affairs of government were willing to risk England to still anxieties aroused by the possible spread of communism. Fearing the loss of empire, mayhem of empire, they have dealt as a brutal father with the peoples of India and Ireland. But on the whole the British have not sought the praise of others. They have found satisfaction as well as power in their concerns at home and about the world. Their poets could sing,

"Oh to be in England
Now that April's there"

with indifference as to what the Chinese or the Italians or the Americans might think of an English April. An Englishman's house has been his castle, and each Englishman has had a right to his own particular and peculiar castle.

The same defects of economic inequality have persisted in England as elsewhere, but the sons who did not have John Bull's blessing could speak bluntly to their father about it. The prime minister himself was not immune from the requirement to answer publicly why the government had or had not done any particular act or pursued any course. (The symbol of the supreme father remained, however, immune in the person of the king.) At home in his island castle, at least, the British as a nation have progressed far toward that maturity which must exist for the realization of democracy.

So we can see that the search for equality, which is inherent in the democratic faith, has deep psychological roots in man's development to maturity. It is collateral to his attempt to find liberty, that is, to escape from paternalism. It is collateral, too, to his achievement of brotherhood, to a collaboration among equals. The revolutionary slogans, "All men are created equal," and "Liberty, Equality and Fraternity," and that the workers of the world shall unite because they have nothing but their chains to lose are not just political rhetoric. They are expressions of dawning maturity and a call to normal, instinctual development.

3

Competitive Society

THE FOURTH CHAPTER of the Book of Genesis recounts how Cain was angry because the Lord had not respect for his offering, whereas the offering of Cain's younger brother Abel had been respected. "And the Lord said unto Cain, Why art thou wroth? and why is thy countenance fallen? If thou doest well, shalt thou not be accepted?"

If Cain had found it possible to answer this question in the affirmative, he would not have slain Abel. If society in the past had been able to answer the question with a yes, it would have been less of an arena for power struggles and better adapted to the recognition of individual needs and responsibilities. If we are to progress in our own democracy, this question put to Cain must be effectively answered.

There are two important concepts to be found here: the first, that despair and anger come when one is not accepted, whether it be the individual or the outcast tribe or nation; the second, that if one does a job well, to one's own satisfaction, he will be accepted. This is perhaps the hardest lesson in all life to be learned.

There are numberless examples in history and art of the story of Cain, examples of men and women who suppressed their antagonism toward their younger brothers, and instances also of Jacobs who competed for the birthrights of their elder brothers. The experience of almost everyone illuminates the fear and anger of older children when they must share the affection of their parents with newcomers, with upstarts, with people (youngsters) who express their wants without restraint. We know, too, from family histories the story of these invaders, of these younger children who feel that someone has been ahead of them in harvesting affection. These are the seeds of the combat for power, of the constant pressure to send out tendrils to encompass parental affection and to find sustenance in parental praise. It was a short transference from the blessing of parents to seek this same assurance of regard and strength from tribal elders, who spoke for the departed spirits and the gods, and from them once more to the magician and the priestly orders and those authorities which became the state. "The wrath of a King is as messengers of death; but a wise man will pacify it. In the light of the King's countenance is life; and his favor is as a cloud of the latter rain." It is a small transposition from the purchase of a birthright for a mess of pottage or a venison stew, to the payment of money for an affectionate word or to manipulate one's own life for wealth and the power of wealth in place of parental reward. We continually make such substitutions in vain attempts to retrieve from childhood signs of parental security.

Of course, in primitive times to receive a father's blessing was like receiving his weapon; it was a passing on of the potency of the head of the family or clan; it was symbolized by feasting on his totem. His curse reduced to impotence. One can read that in the attitude of the authors of Greek drama and of the Bible toward one cursed by his father. A replica of this pattern is to be found in the courtier or official who became strong through his sovereign's blessing and very literally impotent when the sovereign's curse removed his head. We see today the blessing of the state in the grant of powers, offices, monopolies, immunities; we know its frown in the form of legal sanctions, outlawry, forfeitures. These patterns of paternalism stem from roots deep in childhood.

Before leaving the stories of Cain and Abel, and Jacob and Esau, we should notice another component feature of both—the guilt of him who succeeded in his power quest. Cain in his guilt tries to hide from God; Jacob is afraid to meet Esau and sends before him rich gifts to buy his peace. In each instance the elimination of the rival does not bring satisfaction; there is neither parental nor fraternal peace secured from the triumphs of superior power of violence, purchase or deception. There is no security when power is the aim of action. The child must forever be reassured; the adult must repeat and repeat each unsuccessful search for satisfaction; the rich man must multiply his fortune; he must make repeated gifts to welfare and charity, to God and his brother Esau; the sovereign must extend his rule and gain the last syllable of recognition; the dictator must make the crescendo of his triumphs faster and bolder.

But let us imagine that Jacob had said, "Why should I begrudge Esau his blessing? My father prefers him but my mother prefers me." What would the results have been? Suppose, in other words, Jacob had accepted the difference between himself and Esau without the necessity of making it a trial of acumen or strength, would he not then have behaved in a manner which we consider more mature? It is not mature to say, "I'll give you my lollipop if you'll let father and mother give me the last good-night kiss"; or even to say, "If you mind your own business and let the government give us large land grants we'll build a railroad to give you jobs and access to markets."

Again, let us assume that Cain had said, "Yes, if I do well I shall be accepted. If I can find satisfaction in my work, in making use of the earth to create things that will satisfy my needs and those of the family that relies on me, then I shall not need a sign of the Lord's acceptance. I shall know in that very satisfaction that I am blessed." Would this not represent a more mature attitude, a more mature civilization, than that expressed in the feeling that his brother must be a competitor and the compulsion to destroy that competitor? Suppose Cain had thought, "After all, my bent is agriculture, Abel's is animal husbandry; there is a place for both of us." Would that not be a greater security for Cain than to feel that he must measure differences against a fantasy of acceptance? Men strain for security, but have they ever found it in aggressive competition or in a failure to accept differentiation as in itself no threat? For if the attempt to find security is made through aggressive competition, then the only good Indian is a dead Indian, and your own scalp is in issue; and if the fact of variation becomes a threat to you, if it arouses fantasies to satisfy your own real or imagined failures, then the sword must be forever in your hand—for if you are a man you will resent woman; if a woman, you will resent man; if you be of the majority faith or race you will fear the minority and vice versa; he who deviates from you will enter into every sentence in your mind, every desire of your heart, like King Charles's head. "He is different; therefore he must have something on me," can be the road to the asylum, the motto of perennial immaturity or the poison of society.

Concurrent with the drive to power, with the aggressive urge to competition, we find the longing for those moments of experience sometimes half-submerged in the subconscious, seemingly a dream, in which the ideal of no competition is realized, in which peace has been earned, or possibly bought. The pretty fantasy persists of each man living quietly under his own vine and fig tree, in his own undisturbed Eden, where no tree bears forbidden fruit and no one threatens interference. Then there will be a great brotherhood of all mankind. David and Jonathan will be as brothers. David, the little fellow who slew the overpowering and threatening giant, and Jonathan, the King's son, will live in peace and brotherly love. The statesman longs to return to his law office, the industrialist to his farm or science laboratory—if only he can get release from his obligations—obligations imposed in large measure through his own search for power satisfaction, burdens which appear to him to be in conflict with noncompetitive contentment. This is not to say that statesmen and industrialists cannot find satisfaction in their work and contentment in their play. But then it must be work and play which in themselves are media for the expression of personal interest and the exercise of personal capacities, not used by men and women as evidence to themselves and the world of their increasing or continued potency. There is no Utopia through dreams, no heaven on earth to be found where men play harps or skittles and women sing like the angels and purr like kittens.

It is the transitory nature of the satisfaction we get from power and glory and the momentary assuaging of bloodlust that requires of those who are insecure in their relations to others a reiteration of cruelty. This keeps the world stirred up. This insecurity is not that economic insecurity on which the Marxists pin their faith, for Croesus himself and the most redoubtable and economically well-founded capitalists have generally been unable to desist from the struggle for greater wealth and power. The manufacturer must expand his plant, the banker must move to control the industries he finances and, where he can, the government whose bonds he buys and notes he discounts. Always these men of power and affairs measure themselves against possible competitors and enemies. Fearing eclipse, they must push on toward monopoly and complete control, demons more unattainable than any god. This is the dilemma of power and glory and of the use of all three weapons of the power struggle, that is, violence (i.e. the slaying of Abel), economic power (i.e. the purchase of a birthright for a mess of pottage) and control over the mind and emotions (i.e. securing the birthright by misrepresenting Jacob as Esau).

If the only choice of mankind lay between the Utopian dream and the bite of power, no vestige of hope for maturity would remain, no scintilla of expectation for civilization. But the fact is that individual men and women do become mature, and a third alternative for social man exists in the hypothesis that a sufficiently substantial part of mankind can become mature enough to recognize the fallacies of both the compulsive struggle for power and the fantasy of Arcadian bliss, the fallacies that satisfaction can be achieved by aggression and destruction on the one hand or getting everything for nothing on the other. There is hope in the hypothesis that, once men recognize the way to maturity, there will be a sufficient number of them ready to pursue that way to colonize and expand the new world.

This hope has long ago been translated into basic ethical doctrine. It is the core of the concept of brotherly love, of brotherly equality as against fraternal competition. It is the heart of the admonition to love thy neighbor as thyself, in contrast to fearing that in difference there lies danger and competitive destruction (or, as Paul wrote to the Galatians, "Thou shalt love thy neighbor as thyself. But if ye bite and devour one another, take heed that ye be not consumed one of another"). In this hope of maturity is the seed of the program to do unto others as you would have them do to you, rather than to attempt to acquire power over them. It is the impulse leading to the social objective of requiring of each man according to his ability and rendering to each according to his need in comparison with getting what you can, when you can, while the getting's good. It is the kernel of philosophies such as those of the Stoics, the Quakers and the Chinese, emphasizing the integrity of individual man.

The ethical pattern of family life is not competitive. When it is, there is discord in the family. Instead of competition we grant to each member of the family according to his needs and ask from each according to his ability. The breadwinner does not eat all the bread because he earns it, or because he has greater strength or holds the purse strings. The core of what we know as civilization is in the increasing achievement of this pattern of shared equality in family life and its extension to other social connections. The family relationship to property is far more than an equality of property rights or even a community interest in property. As a matter of law, neither such equality nor community interest may exist. But it is an ethical and psychological attitude which grants respect for the weaker members and their needs and shares responsibility among the members in accordance with their capacities. It is a fellowship and not a prison or a prize ring.

The problem of democratic living is not greatly different from the problem of good family life. It cannot be based on terror or greed, on cruelty or selfishness, if the several members are to develop their capacities and are not to be hampered by a sense of impending threat or illusions of personal impotence. Children do not mature in such an atmosphere nor parents realize the fullness of their maturity. In the good home mutual respect and understanding develop—not identity either of interest or behavior or capacity or beliefs, nor even of need and satisfaction. In the good society, the happy state, there need not be, nor can there be expected to be, such identity among the members.

In the well-adjusted home there is an ever-expanding equality as the younger members mature, a willingness to share and contribute to the group welfare, a readiness to yield authority and grant independence to the adolescent members, not keep them subordinate as a symbol of parental authority. Its standards of satisfaction are not phrased in terms of, "What can I get?" but rather "What can I do?" Ethical well-being is not parallel to, but identical with, psychological well-being.

But are the same relationships, is the same or a similar fellowship possible in society? This question brings up the problem of the individual in the group larger than the family group. There is a common notion that the individual is *against* society, that freedom and social control are inevitably in conflict. It is sometimes suggested that individual man is by nature a free being, and that he must forever expend his energies trying to free himself from the throttling effect of society. The eighteenth-century social philosophers were convinced that the happy savage was a free being corrupted by society against Natural Law. If only he could live on a desert island, or even a farm, he would be free of society and could live a normal life. But could he? Has man ever escaped the influence of a social group?

We know man only as a social animal. It is as fantastic to conceive of him apart from a social group as it is to imagine him without the law of gravity. St. Anthony in the desert and Peary at the North Pole had not escaped society. Your hermit is affected by society, for he is the neurotic who cannot adjust himself to other people and must flee them. To him they are a constant threatening force. He can only quiet his own urge to measure himself and his real or imagined shortcomings by removing himself from the proximity of others against whom and whose real or imagined capacities he is driven to measure himself.

In fact, man is no more apart from or against society than the soloist is apart from or against the orchestra in a concerto. He has his cadenzas in which the orchestra does not participate, the tutti have their passages in which resound the full and mingled voices of the group; but the orchestra does not drown out the soloist nor does the soloist disregard the orchestra in the performance of the concerto. Just so man has individual passages in his life in which no one can share, and society has its great crescendos, in which the individual seems to be swallowed in the mass of voices; but both exist contemporaneously. They mingle together.

The man who acts against society is not inevitably against it. He is either aggressive in his desire to destroy or overthrow some person or group of persons or some institutions, or he is afraid of his aggressive tendencies or tired of the debilitating struggle with others and then attempts to escape the repeated disillusionment and continuous suppression.

We know that, as the child struggles to be accepted as a part of the family group, he is at the same time struggling to be recognized as different from the family group. The son likes to look like Father, but in the same breath he wishes his aunts would say that he is also stronger and bigger. The daughter likes to be told her voice is like her mother's, but she longs to be more beautiful and socially more competent. These urges are not stilled even by the knowledge that a time will come when the son's strength will exceed his father's, the daughter's beauty her mother's. With adolescence the need to show one's own capacity develops with increasing force; one doesn't want to be the

Johnsons' little boy or girl or even big boy or girl; one wants to be Dick Johnson or Anna Johnson. One wants to achieve the interest of others in oneself, not in just a member of the Johnson family. If recognition of this individuality is denied by parents, the adolescent becomes aggressive or passive; his development is distorted.

Dorothy Canfield, in *The Election on Academy Hill*, discusses a conversation between a townsman and a summer visitor. The townsman thinks that the visitor is not like most of them, for he looks right at you when he talks; his eye is not on the next thing or something far away.* It is no vanity that we like to be acknowledged as in ourselves worthy of a look of attention. It is a bridge between our several aspirations and our variations from one another. It is the path to that sharing and communion which enriches experience. The lack of this recognition of individual integrity induces us to compete for acceptance or, failing to achieve it, to withdraw from social intimacy. Here, then, is the root of the feeling that society is against man and that man in defense must see what he can get out of society or damn it by indifference. To such negative attitudes, the democratic postulates which we have made offer a positive approach.

---

* This common habit of ignoring others at the very moment we converse with them is described by Louis Macneice in "Conversation" (*Poems 1925-1940*):

> Ordinary people are peculiar too:
> Watch the vagrant in their eyes
> Who sneaks away while they are talking with you
> Into some black wood behind the skull,
> Following un-, or other, realities,
> Fishing for shadows in a pool.

Recognition by the family group may be sufficient for the adult; it is not enough for young people. The clan may have been enough, but even there the taboos against marriage within the clan must have made for a desire for wider recognition, a desire which must have been frustrated where marriages were arranged by elders. Paternalism may give a good, godlike experience to the patron; but it will scarcely satisfy the young person who wants to go directly to the object of his desires, which may be to his lady or may be to the sun or may be to a school for aviation mechanics.

Beyond family and clan, men have other social relationships—in occupation, recreation, religious observance and political life. In such relationships they may be competitive and seek preferment, or they may ask only that their individualities, their capacities and interests and needs, be not glossed over but noticed with a sympathetic interest. They want to talk about their jobs, their childhood, their families, their health, their opinions and the little things they have observed and what they said then and thereafter.

> Around my fire an evening group to draw,
> And tell of all I felt, and all I saw.

It is here that society has failed. It has not adequately afforded men and women, and young people in particular, such recognition. When the fluid mass of factory workers, typists and salesgirls succeeded the apprentice and journeyman and clerk, the relation of employee to master and owner was changed. Profit replaced livelihood as the purpose of production and commerce. Money-making became abstract: it was abstracted from making a living.

There was little left of normal, healthy recognition of worker. The relationship became more and more that of children competing with each other for a sign of affection from parents and developing aggression toward elders with whom they could not compete and in comparing themselves to whom they felt themselves failures. The sign of affection for which they competed was a job or promotion. They organized themselves into unions to acquire the power of numbers where the satisfactions of personal relations failed. They joined clubs and fraternal organizations where they could be hailed as "Brother" because their lives were devoid of noncompetitive recognition in their other relationships with men.

One reads in the Bible of a struggle for a satisfaction of the same need. Men wanted their own local altars where they could participate in worship and be known by the local congregation. But the priests and the rulers wanted religious worship centralized in Jerusalem; they wanted that unity and its corollary, dependence, which assured them of control. The prophets condemned the corruption which inevitably followed this concentration of power; and Jesus answered the prayer of the common man for recognition by preaching the doctrine that the Lord, the Father, was available to all men wherever they might worship Him.

Whatever the gain in individual freedom of thought and action which the Reformation brought about, it also involved for a large part of the Christian world a depersonalization of religion. For the Catholic churches, while making reliance upon them and the intercession of Christ and the saints essential to salvation, nevertheless dramatize the importance of the individual through the sacraments. Confession and communion proclaim a sympathetic interest in the individual soul and the way to its salvation.

Political life also has reflected the depersonalization of institutions. The triumph of the royal court over feudalism involved the abrogation of most requirements of service by the tenant to his immediate overlord and protection by that overlord of his tenant. Labor and produce rendered to the overlord was replaced by cash rents and by taxes collected in the name of that distant and unfamiliar enthroned overlord, the king.

The Puritan and French revolutions tended to personalize government again. You might not be a part of government, but some fellows like you who didn't wear silk pants were in seats of the mighty. If you were a French peasant you got the sense that the Revolution recognized that you were a man. You could now work for yourself, and need not slave for the aloof father on the throne and the support of his pompadoured women and crystal chandeliers and absentee landlords. If you were a British tradesman you had the sense that the new government and the new principles of government recognized your personal needs. The American Revolution was among other things a resistance to the tendency to depersonalize the frontiers and make the merchant jump to tunes piped three thousand miles away. The very language—"All men are created equal"—"Liberty, Equality, Fraternity"—and the British policy of protecting a Britain with guns if need be in any part of the world, caused men to feel that they were accepted; they were a part of the government; it was theirs; they were not to be dependent or treated as unruly children.

The local politicians continue to pay attention to the individualities of their constituents. They pat the babies on the head, inquire about Mother's lumbago and try to get jobs for the sons. The political club is a social outlet.

But London and Paris and Washington have been far from the people; and Berlin and Rome after unification as well as before never came close to them. Until recently the affairs of central governments have for the greater part been impersonal—tariffs, currency, armies, colonies. Governments frequently made appeals to the little businessman and the wage-earner, but they had nothing to offer them that made them feel recognized as persons, as individualities. They were only voters and taxpayers. The government looked over their heads, at somebody else, at something else. And only a small proportion of voters generally came or come to the polls. Before the second World War the social service state—in the Scandinavian countries, the United States and the British Commonwealth—had begun to make government more personal. This movement has been overpowered now by the paternalism of the dominating state-at-war.

Politics and administration have become largely a matter for experts. The great corporations which controlled the larger part of production and distribution before the war were not operated by their stockholder-owners, but by technicians in finance, in buying and selling, in manufacturing and administering. With rare exception, such as the Quakers, religion has been guided more by the expert than by the instinct of the parishioner toward God. Even in recreation, individual participation has lagged, and the expert in acting and talking and entertaining has made men sitters instead of doers; we have divorced the use of the mind and skill and personal cleverness from the fun of millions of people. Professionalized sports have substituted enduring seats for strong muscles.

It is sometimes difficult to distinguish the expert who controls the instrumentalities of power from the instrumentalities of power themselves. This is obvious in the case of the dictator, expert in the field of government. It is apparent also in the realm of the financier who, throughout the early part of the twentieth century, knew the art of floating securities and obtaining funds for that expansion of plant necessary to destroy or minimize competition. It is true also at times of the labor Czar.

Sometimes it is hard to distinguish between expertness and wizardry, and a population unschooled in the niceties of technical knowledge is inclined to accept an expert's word with mind agape, without much thought of who pays the expert or what his moral ends may be. The elders and their wizard are repeated in the men of power and their expert.

There is nothing to indicate that the patterns of individual human behavior change in group relations; for, men being social, their patterns of behavior are necessarily composed of relationships to one or more other individuals. There is a variety of patterns, but none that ignores the existence of other persons. The old maid may have closed her mind to marriage and her heart to man, but man will affect her life and behavior as he did David Copperfield's Aunt Betsy's. The multiplicity of individual patterns gives to the group the aspect of a plaid. It is a new pattern, but the individual is not something apart from the whole.

Man, then, is not separate from society; he is not necessarily opposed to society; rather, he is set in it. But social organization may suppress or threaten to destroy him, and he may then rebel against society. The more we know about the delinquent child, the better do we recognize that he is the offspring of psychological insecurity, the slave of unsatisfied desires to gain acceptance on an infantile level. He feels cheated and believes that every hand is against him. Every institution becomes transposed into an unrequiting parent or a brother who has dispossessed him. He is "against" society; and society, except in recent years in some places, has harried him—but neither freed itself of him nor him of society. The mature man or woman on the other hand, who is ready to accept differences without being thrown into passions of terror or anger, who finds satisfaction in the exercise of his or her capacities, who can share the exercise or the fruits of the exercise of those capacities, does not need praise to produce something or to feel safe. Such a person is never "against" society. Praise and reward will still be sweet but not essential to individual development or satisfaction.

It is in a paternalistic situation, in a repetition of childhood patterns, that praise and rewards are essential. They are necessary to the recipient because they are the measure of paternal affection and the assurance that no beating is in prospect. They must be offered by the patron as insurance against a search for other satisfactions apart from patronage. For when the patronage relationship fails to give satisfaction, satisfactions may be sought in new ways; then man may go against the patron—or society.

Propaganda has set up this supposed antithesis of individual and society as inevitable, propaganda by those who believed that the state that governed least was the one which governed best. To them it appeared obvious that man was against society either because it attempted to interfere with free competition, or because he was jealous of those who possessed worldly goods. The Middle Ages knew no such concept. Man had a place in political and economic life through feudal status; he had a place in spiritual and ethical life in the church. For centuries, until its institutions became chiseled away or corrupted by the seekers after power and privilege, the paternalism of the Middle Ages had a portion to offer in this world and the next to every child—not a good portion, perhaps, in material satisfactions, but he was not left to sink or swim. The same situation was true of primitive societies, which shared among their members what means of subsistence or what famine there was. Men were not hungry while others were affluent. Everyone had his place, and each was respected in his own right.

The struggle for power and for the distribution of the weapons of power does not alone explain the internal and external conflicts of nations, the failure to approach the ideal of fraternity. It is not simply the reaction to an unequal diffusion of economic security in goods and opportunities which brings about attempts to readjust the balance, the reforming and revolutionary periods of history. These struggles and attempts at readjustment are symptoms; they hark back to motivations familiar to us all. We can see the elements of this design in competitive family life; and in family life we can also discover a blueprint for the achievement of satisfaction.

It would appear, consequently, that as the ethical concepts of society place man in social relationships which involve social responsibilities, they concur with those psychological factors which are involved in maturity.

To do a job well for the satisfaction of self-realization or because it makes possible the satisfaction of other needs in various relationships—to carry on satisfactorily relationships of reciprocity with family, friends and acquaintances—these are the aims of the good life, whether framed in terms of psychological maturity or ethical principles; or when paraphrased in terms of fraternity or democracy. But ethical ends tend to be garbled and psychological growth squeezed out where competition is the keynote, where the drive is to beat up or beat out someone else, either in fact or symbolically or even by straining to attain the power to do so.

It would follow that ethical ends cannot be divorced from a recognition of their psychological components. They cannot be attained without a program that proceeds towards aiding more and more people to achieve emotional and intellectual maturity. What mechanism will tend to forward such maturity?

Part II

SOME PROBLEMS OF DEMOCRACY

4

What Is This Thing Democracy?

IN THE MIDDLE-WESTERN village of Buffunville, certain questions perplexed the community. There was considerable disagreement which gave rise to hard feeling and occasionally on Saturday nights to fisticuffs. To settle the matter the Buffunville *News & Vilifier* proposed that a mass meeting of all the townspeople be held at the local baseball field to dispose of the problems in the good old democratic way by majority vote. This proposal met with such general acclaim that the mayor called the meeting, and the townsfolk gathered on the diamond to perform a democratic rite. Every question would be put to a vote and the majority would win, because, of course, democracy is majority rule.

There were not enough seats for all, so the Negroes present were required to stand. No one would sit in the same row with the Jewish storekeeper and his family until all the other seats were taken. The owner of the leading industry in town had brought his twenty employees and their families in the school bus. It was said he had told his people to vote right or look for another job.

The questions to be voted on were three:

(1) Did the village books balance correctly?
(2) Were those who believed in the Darwinian theory and advocated the teaching of that theory in the schools unpatriotic?
(3) Should a man whose wife bore triplets be run out of town because they had increased the costs of child health service and the public school?

When the meeting opened a dour chap of New England ancestry, who was the town lawyer and read the Declaration of Independence aloud from the steps of the village office to all who would listen every Fourth of July, arose and said: "Mr. Mayor, I rise to question whether the democratic process of voting can possibly determine whether books are in balance, whether the theory of evolution is correct or whether a man should be driven from his wife and children."

By majority vote it was thereupon decided that the majority could do all these things because that was democratic.

Then the dour chap stood up again and said: "Mr. Mayor, I rise to question whether a meeting is democratic which segregates a part of the community and where more than forty votes are controlled by one man."

The matter was not put to a vote, but, in the words of the Buffunville *News & Vilifier*, "Two good citizens (i. e., the truck drivers for the factory) ejected the disreputable pettifogger from the ball park."

What Is This Thing Democracy?

The question remains, who was right? What is democracy?

The very fact that again and again we ask ourselves and each other, "What do you mean by democracy?" demonstrates our uncertainty as to what we expect. Is it majority rule? We are told so by politicians, labor leaders and men and women of every political faith and occupation. That is a common definition. Is democracy free speech, free press, all the other civil rights, perhaps together with the other freedoms included in Mr. Roosevelt's four freedoms? This is the essence of the democratic recipe, we are told by liberals. Then from the universities and schools of social work comes the suggestion that democracy is a way of life, that it infuses all of our hours, even those in which we are not at the polls or seeking the protection of our constitutional liberties.

Doubtless democracy is something of all of these and more. Certainly it has enough of each of these ingredients to deceive us into believing that, having distinguished the element to which we are particularly sensitive, we have found the full formula. It is as though we were to describe a school by the teachers or the books or the children or the benches, when, of course, the school is all of these but more. What counts most is the purpose of teachers and pupils and the attitude of teachers and pupils towards one another and towards the books and the benches and learning and the life of the school too. Similarly, it is ends and attitudes that count for most in community life and make a community democratic or something else.

Let us revert to the assumptions concerning democracy

which were made in the foreword. Let us consider our problem from the base of those assumptions. They were that the democratic principle involves: (1) Respect for individuals and the variations among individuals, their needs and their aspirations. (2) Making possible equal opportunity for every individual to obtain satisfaction by realizing and exercising his capacities and pursuing his interests. (3) Equality of treatment of each individual by those with power or authority. (4) The concept that equality does not mean identity, but rather recognition of differences, a recognition of differences not in the form of favoritism, but as an expression of respect for individuality. (5) Collaboration, rather than competition or paternalism as the more likely method for achieving mutual respect, equality and development.

The validity of these assumptions as a social program is to be found in that they satisfy the ethical ends of society which have been set forth as desirable by peoples throughout the world for thousands of years, and in that they conform to the psychological needs of men and women in the development of their maturity. We shall see, too, that no definition of democracy is complete or satisfactory without the inclusion of these assumptions.

From Moses and Jesus and Confucius comes the concept of equality, not expressed idly as something desirable which, if realized at all, will come about by itself or through prayer, but in terms of individual behavior and responsibility. From Buddha and Lao-tse and Saint Francis comes the corollary of charity, of the surrender of privilege, of the satisfactions to be realized through sharing. Socrates seeking for justice and the Stoics for a way of life have also found the keystone to ethical social behavior in the dignity of the individual man, in man who for all his irrational conduct is a being capable of reason. In *Fountainheads of Freedom*, Irwin Edman writes:

> The Stoics emphasized the sense of human dignity and self-sufficiency in the face of pain or pleasure, and in the face of all social collapse.

He quotes from the *Meditations* of Marcus Aurelius:

> Never value anything as profitable to thyself which shall compel thee to break thy promise, to lose thy self-respect, to hate any man, to suspect, to curse, to act the hypocrite, to desire anything which needs walls and curtains: for he who has preferred to everything else his own intelligence and daemon and the worship of its excellence, acts no tragic part, does not groan, will not need either solitude or much company; and, what is chief of all, he will live without either pursuing or flying from death . . . taking care of this only all through life, that his thoughts turn not away from anything which belongs to an intelligent animal and a member of a civil community.

Here is an adult philosophy which recognizes human dignity under all conditions, self-respect and respect for human intelligence, which does not ask for rewards and punishments as a guide to conduct or an inspiration to sound relations with other persons.

Whatever the inequalities of political and economic life may have been, in religious tradition men have for thousands of years deemed themselves equal before God, the Supreme Father. In religious faith every man has been deemed respected for himself, not *en masse,* before God; every man has been held entitled to treatment according to his deserts, not necessarily identically with other men; and every man has been recognized as having equal opportunity to achieve salvation as an individual.

Man has instinctively, or through divine inspiration, if you will, dreamed of a day in which social and economic distinctions will be neutralized and political power will not be arbitrarily used. Men have feared immediate danger to themselves if they should take action leading to greater equality. They have closed their eyes even to their own acts which have brought about their greater enslavement. Nevertheless, again and again men have revered the men of old and worshiped the heroism of those who sacrificed themselves so that others might be free to enjoy greater equality, and through equality realize more satisfactory lives. Men have worshiped those who have sacrificed themselves in the interest of the common humanity of ordinary individuals.

Not only are the ethical ends of society satisfied by our assumptions as to the nature of democracy, but those assumptions also meet the demands of the normal psychological growth of mankind. We have seen how the development of the child involves the emergence of the individual from a state of identification to a stage of recognition of the separate individualities of himself and those with whom he is in contact. In society there is a parallel development in which personal integrity is recognized, and new categories of people achieve equality with those who had previously assumed a paternalistic role.

Throughout the greater part of the historical period, men have identified institutions with the persons who had power through those institutions. Those without power rarely hazarded the thought that institutions were for common men to make of what they would. C. H. McIlwain makes this clear. In discussing the classical ancient world he tells us in *The Growth of Political Thought in the West*, quoting *De Legibus:*

> To a Greek thinking politically, an oligarchy or a king *was* the state; to a Roman thinking in terms of law, it was "the proper business of the magistrate to understand that he impersonates the state to maintain its due honor and dignity, to conserve its laws, to administer its rights and to be reminded of the things committed to his trust."

This development from Greek identification of the state with its governor to the Roman symbolism by which those in authority stood for or impersonated the state intrusted to them, was a necessary first step. It led through the equality of citizenship in the Augustinian City of God to principles of political equality expressed in the Declaration of Independence and the Declaration of the Rights of Man.

Dictatorship is a throwback to the identification of the state with the men in power. But lesser examples of this identification are familiar to us in the form of the political boss, the powerful industrialist and the labor oligarch.

Just as in the individual development from childish identification to the more adult recognition of the equality of individuals, so with the abandonment of the identification of ruler and state there has been the historical change in attitude towards the equality of people. A. J. Carlyle says in *A History of Medieval Political Theory in the West:*

> There is no change in political theory so startling in its completeness as the change from the theory of Aristotle to the later philosophical view represented by Cicero and Seneca. Over against Aristotle's view of the natural inequality of human nature we find set out the theory of the natural equality of human nature.

In the struggle between those who seek equality and those who must deny it to maintain their own sense of strength and manhood, the weapons of force, wealth and propaganda are used to suppress or destroy. In the course of the contest over the continuance of paternalistic controls, the weapons and the minds of the men who use them tend to become fixed on side-issues rather than on the basic struggle. Life then becomes a series of competitive engagements to assure the contestants of their strength or their prestige—that is, that reputation for power which will make its actual trial an unnecessary test. In this competitive engagement the end is generally concealed, and the proof of success is not an acknowledgment of equality, not a mature inner strength and conviction of equality. That purpose is lost, and those who begin by seeking equality pass over to accepting a prize, a reward. It is not enough to live well; one must keep up with the Joneses or even have something that they lack. So also competition leads men away from the path to self-development by the flattery of praise from men with superior wealth or power. The small manufacturer is satisfied by orders from the great automobile plant. Men of little learning or skill are flattered by honorary degrees from universities, or by positions of honor but of little trust. In these circumstances, the flight from paternalism goes just so far and then, adolescent-like, the rebel asks a sign of paternal grace.

We have also noticed that, concurrent with the drive to escape from paternalism and to assume the place of an equal, is the drive towards fraternity, towards finding acceptance and towards sharing or participating. It is true that the achievement of brotherhood is time and again interrupted by suspicion, by the fear of being fraternally imposed upon as one was, perhaps, as a child. We may accept intellectually the thesis of the equality of persons of another race; we may in our minds feel prepared to join as in brotherhood some co-operative venture with men of different background from our own; but we are blocked because emotionally we still cling to patterns, in part of threads from the nursery, woven into our persons. We cannot easily let down the barriers which our childhood created for our defense and find the common interest we may have with others or give to them something of our humane and creative selves.

Nevertheless, neither our failures to grow out of paternalism, nor to free others from our own control, nor our failures to build in brotherhood belie the theme of our development. For all its discords and failures, this moves towards a climax of freedom from control by others, towards equality with others in the realization of our opportunities, and towards fraternally creating and sharing. In spite of all our atavism, our throwbacks, our civilization tends to move away from relationships based on aggressive competition for power.

Returning to our assumptions as to what is involved in the democratic principle, we must acknowledge that they are in accord with the stream of psychological growth. Respect for individuals and their variations is the first lesson the child must learn as it acquires a consciousness of its own individuality and commences to overcome its identity with the other members of the family. A similar sense of respect on the part of elders for the child is the best atmosphere in which the child can grow to maturity. Such mutual respect is necessary in any community in which the members are to be free to develop and not remain subject to the power of a part of the community or outsiders. It is essential, too, if they are not to eat out their peace of heart in aggression towards each other, if, in the phrase of Wordsworth, they are not to lay waste their power by getting and spending.

The reason for this urge for the respect of individuals and the variations among them, is that only through such mutual respect is it possible for each person to experience for himself, and those dear to him, equal opportunity for the realization of his capacities and interests and the satisfaction of his needs. In a paternalistic situation, where opportunities can be arbitrarily granted or withheld, granted or withheld to meet the needs of the person in the position of dominance, there can be no equality and self-realization, and satisfaction must remain circumscribed by the choices and prejudices of the paternal power. Father can deny **Jenny the opportunity to study art. The Polish govern-**

ment could deny Jews the right to sell tobacco or work on street railroads. The dictatorships can suppress all art, all philosophy, all science that reflect upon or challenge their theses of social order. The music of Shostakovitch may be patriotic today, although yesterday it was taboo as being "left deviationist." All this is paternalism with a vengeance.

Yet everyone has the need to find satisfaction of hungers and of urges to gain security; and the means by which each of us finds satisfaction is influenced by the luxuriant variety of human taste and capacity and environment and experience. Thus, everyone whose spirit is not psychologically deformed and whose abilities are not to be wasted, must develop himself in those ways which his capacities and interests direct. Otherwise he wears a martingale so that he is forced to abandon the pace natural to him for the bowed head and genuflexions which please the master who holds the reins.

Of course, if those with power and authority do not treat others with equality, the theme of the story of Joseph's coat of many colors is revived on each occasion. The man with authority must be hurt. The person who receives his favor must be eliminated. Discrimination is incitement to aggressive competition; it stirs up warfare in the nursery; it diverts the energies of men and women from satisfaction of their needs through self-development to a frantic attempt to obtain a sense of security by attaining rewards or achieving power over others.

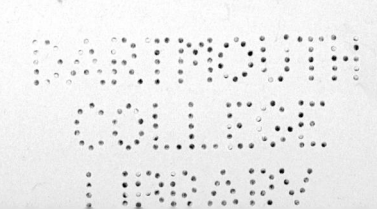

A recognition of equality—which is not confused with identity but recognizes the differences between individuals—is, as we have seen, fundamental to human achievement of maturity. To assure equality of nutrition does not mean that everyone must eat meat on Fridays or pork chops on Saturdays, and that there must be potatoes in a universal diet regardless of the needs of sufferers from diabetes or superfluous weight. The question of equality is not whether all people are to be given an opportunity to be radio announcers, but rather whether all people who desire it will be given a chance to discover whether they are qualified to be radio announcers and, if they are, to develop and use those talents in radio announcing or some other field relevant to their talents; if not, that they get an opportunity to develop such talents as they may have.

Acknowledgment of differences should not be availed of as an excuse for the paternalistic practice of playing favorites, of granting rewards to supporters and punishing opponents. This is again merely incitement to those aggressions which entrench inequality and set in motion the circuit of insecurity and competition for power or the show of power. The spoils system of practical politics is adolescent and tends to keep the beneficiaries of such a system in a state of immaturity.

Comparatively few men have become mature to the extent of achieving sufficient security in themselves and satisfaction in the exercise of their faculties to rid themselves of the need to seek security under some form of paternalism and through some kind of rewards—and to have no need to reassure themselves by aggression or flight. And because they have not acquired sufficient security and confidence to live by the Golden Rule, they have never fully experienced democracy. It lies, however, only in the mouths of cynics to decry democracy on this account; and cynics are notoriously disillusioned people who have never found in achievement a satisfaction for a loss of security they once had in paternalism.

As the development of democracy involves a continual struggle against paternalism and aggression and the emergence of self-motivated individuals joined in a society that respects individuality, it cannot be forced on others. As Gandhi puts it: "I hold that democracy cannot be evolved by forcible methods. The spirit of democracy cannot be imposed from without; it has to come from within." That is why those who hold the democratic faith must be patient.

To say to a young person, "Now you're of age, behave as a grownup," may give some satisfaction to him, but it does not automatically rid him of childish fears and drives to find security by aggression or by a search for rewards or by a return to parental protection. The progress of growth is slow and not all in a straight line. Neither can authority declare democracy out of chaos and reasonably expect that it will be thereby created. No people got democracy through adopting a constitution or promulgating a bill of rights. The old American fetish of passing a law will not make people democratic. Moreover, to accept democracy on faith or authority would be a contradiction, because the achievement of democracy involves casting off paternalistic authority and the acceptance of mutual responsibility. It necessitates, if not a democratic experience similar to the religious experience of the mystic, at least an individual consciousness of human motivations and a consecration to moral ends.

Nevertheless, in common parlance, people talk as though democracy were an established situation, finished by revolutions in previous centuries, albeit threatened by foreign powers in the same way that the Bourbon or the Hapsburg dynasties were once threatened by foreign powers. As the Lord after six days of labor at the Creation rested on the seventh day, so those who dwell in democratic countries feel that they can rest after the creation of democratic institutions. They assume that there is a finality to those institutions so long as no outsider challenges them —unless it be that they cry out in fright that some new tax or government regulation which challenges their security is a threat not only to themselves but to democratic government. The National Association of Manufacturers, for example, may urge that democracy is endangered by social legislation; it may point to the paternalistic plans of its members as being endangered by such legislation; but in doing so, it shows no awareness of the dynamic character of democracy or of any acceptance of the principle of mutual responsibility of all parts of the population. But to those who accept the faith of democracy there can be no sabbath in pursuing it.

Democracy in the modern world, as we know, was part and parcel of the development of capitalism and science and freedom of thought. It supplied the political mechanism and an ideology for the growth of capitalism, science and freedom of thought; but it was not viewed without suspicion. For the very liberating forces which helped to free men from the paternalistic state of the mercantile era and the paternalistic Church of medieval times would, if followed to their logical conclusions, tend to destroy the paternalism of the capitalist system.

The fear of democracy was openly expressed by the

framers of the American Constitution, by the great political writers of Great Britain and by the statesmen of both lands. Some put it frankly as the fear of the have-nots. Some spoke of the danger of entrusting political (or economic) power to ignorant and passionate masses. Some, bolstered by the classic intellectual snobbery of Plato's *Republic*, proclaimed that only the literate, the educated, were competent to rule—and literacy and education were in those days a virtual monopoly of men of estate.

Hamilton, spokesman of the commercial and financial interests, felt certain that the new government could not be controlled by others than the landowners, merchants and members of the learned professions. In *The Federalist* he wrote:

> We have seen . . . that from the natural operation of the different interests and views of the various classes of the community, whether the representation of the people be more or less numerous, it will consist almost entirely of proprietors of land, of merchants, and of members of the learned professions, who will truly represent all those different interests and views. If it should be objected that we have seen other descriptions of men in the local legislatures, I answer that it is admitted there are exceptions to the rule, but not in sufficient number to influence the general complexion or character of the government.

We see this same conflict clearly expressed in the Putney debates in Cromwell's army in 1647. Colonel Rainborough, speaking for the common soldiers, said:

> For really I think that the poorest he that is in England hath a life to live, as the greatest he; and therefore truly, sir, I think it's clear, that every man that is to live under a government ought first by his own consent put himself under that government.

Ireton, the son-in-law of Cromwell, replied in part as follows:

> ... I think that no person hath a right to an interest or share in the disposing of the affairs of the Kingdom, and in determining or choosing those that shall determine what laws we shall be ruled by here—no person hath a right to this, that hath not a permanent fixed interest in this Kingdom, and those persons together are properly the represented of this Kingdom, and consequently are (also) to make up the representatives of this Kingdom, who taken together do comprehend whatsoever is of real or permanent interest in the Kingdom. . . .
>
> ... I am sure if we look upon that which is the utmost (within [any] man's view) of what was originally the constitution of this Kingdom, upon that which is most radical and fundamental, and which if you take it away, there is no man hath any land, any goods, (or) any civil interest, that is this: that those that choose the representers for the making of laws by which this state and Kingdom are to be governed, are the persons who, taken together, do comprehend the local interest of this Kingdom; that is, the persons in whom all land lies, and those in corporations in whom all trading lies. This is the most fundamental

constitution of this Kingdom and (that) which if you do not allow, you allow none at all. . . .

Then later in the course of the discussion Sexby, speaking for the soldiers, said:

> There are many thousands of us soldiers that have ventured our lives; we have had little propriety in the Kingdom as to our estates, yet we have had a birthright. But it seems now, except a man hath a fixed estate in this Kingdom, he hath no right in this Kingdom. I wonder we were so much deceived. If we had not a right to the Kingdom, we were mere mercenary soldiers.

It should also be noted that the democracy of the fathers of our republic was conceived in terms of Athenian democracy infiltrated by the practices of the New England town meeting. In Athens democracy meant the rule of the many as opposed to oligarchy, the rule of the few. But the many who ruled Athens were a prescribed class of citizens whose ancestors had farmed the hills and valleys of Attica and grazed their herds among them for generations. The slaves and the foreign merchants who were settled in Athens, and even their children and grandchildren born in the city state, who formed the great majority of people living there, could take no part in the government and had no voice in its affairs.

Thus in America and Great Britain the recognition of classes of citizens and limitations on the right to vote and to participate in government was a concept based on the authority of ancient Greece, which was only relatively democratic when not actually oligarchic or monarchic.

"The theory of the natural equality of human nature" had not been accepted in spite of the brave words of the Declaration of Independence that all men were created equal. To the landed squires and the men of commerce who were the backbone of the Anglo-American state, a limited democracy was adequate, for it avoided dynastic tyranny and mob rule. This is made clear by *The Federalist* and other federalist writings of the period. A vestigial remain of this attitude is to be found in the poll tax still used in some of our states as a prerequisite to the right to vote. This serves to disenfranchise not only Negroes, but also the poor whites, that part of the population which is feared by those in control.

In addition, democracy was conceived as essentially local in character. The British have not been willing to admit the capacity of all men off of British soil to govern themselves. The Americans of the eighteenth century doubted the ability of federal government to act without interference with local customs and prejudices. So Jefferson, in attempting to protect the rights of men in a democracy, emphasized the right of home rule in the tenth amendment to the Constitution, which he proposed.

Our modern democratic governments were initiated between two fears: the one that the "mob," the uncontrollable, emotional, illiterate, non-taxpaying majority, might escape the paternalism of landed squire and merchant prince; and the other that unknown men at a distance might control or patronize the local squire and merchant.

Nor was this an isolated historical phenomenon. The Free Cities of medieval times were in much the same position, the merchant guilds fearing equally the mob and the

Emperor. The citizens of the Greek city republics dreaded mob rule and domination by other cities with which they might federate. More recently the little dictators of the Latin American nations have feared their peons and the patronage of the United States. And the history of President Wilson's League of Nations is the story of governments and people torn between a terror of communism and a fear of a superstate.

Having discussed the meaning of democracy in terms of human conduct and ideals, let us consider some of the definitions of democracy mentioned at the beginning of this chapter. Under the "majority rule" doctrine of democracy, our legislatures have purported to pass on the truth of scientific theory, as in the famous instance when the Tennessee legislature outlawed the teaching of Darwinism. Legislatures have interfered with the personal habits of people, as they did notoriously by prohibiting the sale of alcoholic beverages. They have even excluded a majority of people from having a voice in the government of some of our southern states. In other words, majority rule and representative government have been used as a method of determining technical fact or theory, of interfering with the habits of men and women and of proscribing part of the population from participation in the machinery of majority rule.

It is also assumed that majority rule is of itself sufficient justification for the coercion of dissenters.

> Then a majority—in accordance with the democratic principle of majority rule—seek through the

union shop to "coerce" a minority of their fellow workers into union membership at the penalty of discharge.

Thus Golden and Ruttenberg write in *The Dynamics of Industrial Democracy*. Rather than being in accord with a democratic principle, this is an admission of the failure of democratic techniques of collaboration; and when coercion is exercised by a majority against a minority in the union, may it not belie democracy?

By this doctrine, when carried one step further, the government is expected to coerce in the name of the majority. Except where such coercion is an impartial exercise of force against irresponsible anti-social persons such as common criminals, the appeal to government to coerce minorities is the pattern of the appeal to father or the big brother to suppress a little brother.

Surely, if majority rule is to be the test of democracy, there cannot be democracy where anyone is excluded from the franchise or where a majority or a minority purports to deprive all others of a livelihood. How can democracy be differentiated from tyranny if it purports arbitrarily to settle matters of conscience or technical fact through majority vote? Is "the principle of majority rule" any more than a method of majority rule, a technique for finding the resultant of numberless individual wills and desires? Once that resultant is discovered, are there not limits to the action that can flow from it?

Thoreau wrote in his *Civil Disobedience:*

> After all, the practical reason why, when power is once in the hands of the people, a majority are per-

mitted, and for a long period continue, to rule is not because they are most likely to be in the right, nor because this seems fairest to the minority, but because they are physically the strongest. But a government in which the majority rule in all cases cannot be based on justice, even as far as men understand it. . . . Must the citizen ever for a moment, or in the least degree, resign his conscience to the legislator?

Surely if we accept the hypothesis of democracy set forth above, then the majority should respect the individualities and variations among dissenters and minorities —it cannot treat all people as identical. Perhaps the minority will prove to be right. Then it ought to be possible for the minority to become a majority. So the machinery of a government dedicated to the recognition of the integrity of individuals must provide for auditing the words and acts, not just of minority groups, but also of majorities and of those who hold the major weapons of sovereignty. Except under dictatorships we do not recognize any more the doctrine that the king can do no wrong. Just as parents can do wrong, so can governors; just as gangs of criminals can be destructive, so can majorities and those who act on the mandate of majorities. Free speech and press and assembly are, therefore, not merely outlets for individual expression of needs; they are weapons in the armory of sovereignty to gain recognition of those needs. They are weapons of propaganda which over time in many instances have adjusted the balance of power between majorities and minorities.

What we really mean by majority rule is two things:

the first, that in general the majority has the power, if it will, to enforce its views or desires upon the minority; the second, that if human beings are going to coerce one another, it is better to have most of them in agreement as to what policies shall be enforced than to entrust such power to a minority, however wise that minority may appear to be.

Even where it appears necessary, coercion should not be the result of majority rule except on principles laid down in advance—that is, by law or rule. Where facts must be considered, a mechanism must be provided for fact finding, otherwise majority rule may be no more than lynch law, without justice and based solely on emotional considerations of wrath or panic. In such a situation there is no participation by equals; there is again the situation of the older sons of Jacob ganging together against Joseph, the minority.

In Quaker practice no vote is taken, but action only follows a consensus of opinion after each member of the meeting has had an opportunity to express his views. Many times the apparent majority will convince dissenters to accept their view or vice versa, but action is not forced over substantial dissent. There are no coerced votes, no victories by small margins, no glorification of power. This is a matter of attitude. It is an ideal of mutually respectful procedure. This Quaker practice is truly respect for individuality: it is democracy because it represents consensus, *not* majority rule; respect, not coercion.

Civil rights or the four freedoms are also principally mechanisms for the achievement of democracy. They are defenses against tyranny and oppression. They are weapons for securing freedom from those restrictions that prevent the development of men and women. But they are also something more, because free expression, freedom of worship and freedom from want and fear are, in addition, a partial recognition of individual needs. They are part of the living process of self-development. Freedom from want and fear of themselves remove some of those conflicts and impulses which lead to aggression and the demand for rewards and punishment. Free speech, freedom of worship, the right to be critical of those in power are themselves a partial realization of capacities and interests, are a satisfaction of basic individual needs.

However, in more senses than one, one may ask with Gandhi whether the four freedoms include "the freedom to be free."

When we speak of democracy as a way of life, we want to ask, "What way of life? A way to what ends?" Surely, not just a democratic way of life, for that is to define the definition by itself. If it be a way of life, it is a way of life in the sense that it is a pattern for achieving those satisfactions which by our hypothesis we call democratic. To speak of it otherwise, as just a way of life rather than a means to the end of satisfying human needs, is to treat democracy as something static, or perhaps aimless, or relevant to an abstract sort of life rather than a life of individuals. It is good to have a fig tree beneath which to sit, but just sitting and plucking the fruit is not satisfactory. As a way of life it doesn't meet the needs of men to realize and express their capacities or to find security.

So, although the common conceptions of democracy all contain elements of it, they are not complete. Any theory of democracy must include more than its machinery and more than generalities. It must recognize the psychological and ethical ends of man, the basic motivations of his life. We must continually remind ourselves, too, that when we speak of a democracy, we speak only in comparative terms; we speak of a social situation in which people are struggling to free themselves of paternalism and thereby to realize the benefits of equality and the satisfactions of fraternity.

5

Doctor, Mammoth and Co-operative Society

THE DOCTOR OF PHILOSOPHY, the doctor of science, the doctor of medicine and the lawyer hankering for an LL.D. fill cubbyhole offices and scatter about the countryside today in the name of government and industrial enterprise. From their official rabbit warrens these experts or technicians make regulations which are the equivalent of laws, issue rulings which are tantamount to judicial judgments, transmit orders as imperative as those of the chief executive and extend advice to all interested persons on every variety of subject. They are neither cause nor effect of the elephantiasis of government and industry, the growth to mammoth proportions of central government and monopolistic production; rather, they are an inextricable part of that growth. Government and industry would exist without these experts and technicians, but government would be performing different functions and industry would be simpler, humbler and less mechanized.

How horrified and terrified the fathers of American democracy and of British *laissez faire* would have been could they have anticipated this development. Jefferson and Madison, Adam Smith and Jeremy Bentham were interested in men and the humane development of their individual capacities. They believed that these could be realized by intimate contact with affairs and personal conduct of business enterprise. And now government and industry tend to be so large and far out of reach, and the whisper of the technician is amplified into a shout, "I am the expert. Are you going to tell me how to practice my profession? Woe unto you if you disregard my science." Or perhaps simply, "We have studied this problem. We have ruled. Now obey, desist, do what we say—or else."

What a change has taken place since Woodrow Wilson wrote on *The Study of Administration* in 1886:

> The English race, consequently, has long and successfully studied the art of curbing executive power to the constant neglect of the art of perfecting executive methods. It has exercised itself much more in controlling than in energizing government. It has been more concerned to render government just and moderate than to make it facile, well-ordered, and effective. [Other peoples developed administration more rapidly than did the English and American. Nevertheless,] We should not like to have had Prussia's history for the sake of having Prussia's administrative skill; and Prussia's particular system of administration would quite suffocate us. It is better to be untrained and free than to be servile and systematic.

In the face of the evidence brought forth by the successors of the Prussian administrators, it is unlikely that the untrained can remain free today. A similar lesson has been taught us in domestic affairs, for the economic freedom of untrained millions and the independence of an untrained government itself have been threatened by the trained experts on the pay rolls of industry and banking.

Of course, Wilson himself never believed that an expert and effective administrative system must lead to servility. If our reasons are sound and our attitudes healthy, we can afford to borrow from the administrative techniques even of an administrative system which would suffocate us.

> If I see a murderous fellow sharpening a knife cleverly [Wilson said], I can borrow his way of sharpening the knife without borrowing his probable intention to commit murder with it; and so, if I see a monarchist dyed in the wool managing a public bureau well, I can learn his business methods without changing one of my republican spots. He may serve his king; I will continue to serve the people; but I should like to serve my sovereign as well as he serves his.

This is what Wilson did as President. In the first World War he borrowed from the continental powers some of their methods for sharpening a nation at war; he built up a concentration of administrative power. But through the new income tax and the Federal Reserve System he also contributed toward a centralization of power in the federal government and a development of administrative boards not limited to the uses of war. So this leader of the party dedicated to the maintenance of states' rights—as did his predecessors, Jefferson in the Louisiana Purchase and Cleveland, who invoked the use of federal troops and the federal injunction in a labor dispute—gave impetus to the eclipse of the states by the national government.

What are the doctors and the mammoths doing to those social attributes and institutions, those human urges and needs involved in the creation of a democratic and co-operative society? Does size and expertness necessarily lead to a new paternalism? Must the fraternity of men and women bow to men in the laboratories, the statistical bureaus and the college lecture halls as people once did to royalty and now do to tyrants? Is there a place for a co-operative society of equals in the face of men who understand electrodynamics, biochemistry, tax yields, the construction of super power dams and psychiatry?

In *The School for Dictators*, Ignazio Silone sets forth a test for the diagnosis of the health of a democracy:

> The first test to be applied in judging an alleged democracy is the degree of self-government attained by its local institutions. If the master's rule in the factory is absolute, if the trade-unions are controlled by bureaucracies, if the bishop or some family is absolute master of the parish, if a man who eats out of the hand of central headquarters rules the roost in the local branch of the party, if the province is governed by the representative of the central government, there can be no true and complete democracy. Only local government can accustom men to responsibility and

independence, and enable them to take part in the wider life of the state.*

If one wishes, therefore, to find out whether democracy in a given country is in good health or bad, one must not attach excessive importance to the number of votes that the democratic or socialist parties receive, or to the circulation of their papers; but one must discover in what honor local government is held and what spirit prevails in the municipalities, the trade unions, the cooperatives, the schools, the local branches of political parties, the parishes, in fact the public bodies of all kinds to which the ordinary man has access.

If we apply this measure to the institutions in democratic lands today, we shall find worrisome symptoms but also some encouraging ones. Our cynicism with respect to local government and the frequent corruption of local authorities and our discouragement with the cumbersome and ineffectual antiques which persist as local institutions are not the sign of honor which a government of the people deserves.

Nevertheless, in the last two decades progress has been made in many cities and smaller communities in the establishment of sound government through fusion movements, proportional representation and city managers. So, too, there have been reorganizations of state governments and

---

* See Jefferson's statement in his letter to Samuel Kercheval, July 12, 1816; that "by making every citizen an acting member of the government, and in the offices nearest and most interesting to him, will attach him by his strongest feelings to the independence of his country, and its republican constitution."

the beginnings of control over irresponsible township and county government. The master no longer rules the factory as he did; local families rarely are masters of parishes or villages any more; the local political leader in general has lost much of the authority he had ten years ago. But many of our larger trade-unions are controlled by bureaucracies, and the arm of central government has stretched out, not so much geographically as functionally, to control commerce and industry, education and welfare.

In a broader sense the test of self-government in local institutions tends to produce even more confusing results. Whereas the power of the federal government has increased greatly in proportion to the state and local governments, the power of the state has diminished in proportion to that of the great urban centers; and, concurrently, new forms of local government have evolved. The political balance was redistributed by such instrumentalities as the Interstate Commerce Commission, the Income Tax, the Federal Reserve Banks and the Reconstruction Finance Corporation.

The Interstate Commerce Commission, in the United States, and the short-lived Poor Law Board established by Act of Parliament of 1834 and the General Board of Health, in Great Britain, led the way to the development of the administrative board. This administrative tribunal has short-cut fact finding, policy making, law enforcement, and the introduction of expert knowledge into governmental activity.

The cumbersome checks and balances afforded by the legislative, administrative and judicial branches of government have been merged in such boards to give greater scope to specialization. Vast fields have been delegated to these so-called "independent" boards and commissions. At the same time the older administrative authorities have also acquired greater powers and regiments of specialists, and none more so than the Treasury through the income tax.

Once this form of taxation was adopted, all other sources of revenue shrank in comparison, and the resources of the federal government increased immeasurably in proportion to those of the states. As a result, Congress was called on to appropriate grants in aid towards pensions, public improvements, schools and other activities which had been deemed functions of the states. These grants were made conditionally and through the enforcement of the conditions the federal government obtained some voice in local affairs. In Great Britain, too, grants-in-aid by Parliament augmented local funds and brought a greater measure of central regulation than even the all-powerful Parliament had been tempted to exercise.

The Federal Reserve System gave to the federal authority a larger measure of control over banking than it had ever had before and complete control over the monetary system. With the organization of the Reconstruction Finance Corporation, the federal government entered a field previously in the hands of private investment bankers, except for sporadic grants by the government to help build up a merchant marine, to construct railroads and similar special enterprises. It has been estimated that shortly before the second World War the RFC directly or indirectly was responsible for two thirds of our domestic financing. Through its subsidiary, the Export-Import Bank, the RFC is in a position to control foreign trade.

Since then the checks of the states on the federal government have decayed, and the balances between state and federal governments have been reset. By the administrative device of the independent boards and by means of its recently acquired economic powers, the federal government has enhanced its authority. This in itself has led people to Washington in preference to the state capitals to get relief. It has taken the dynamic center of government away from the regions, from the localities, to the hands that hold the funds and are not circumscribed by old state boundaries, boundaries in large measure made meaningless by industrial organization, which is countrywide, and by the automobile and airplane. In this slackening of local responsibility there has been a trend toward relieving localities of their obligations because people have become inclined to look beyond mayor and county commissioner and governor to that far-away golden Cathay on the bank of the Potomac.

Of course, there have still been those who argued for "less government in business, and more business in government," who fought each extension of federal authority in the name of Jeffersonian democracy and generally in the interest of *laissez faire* economics. But, as Professor C. E. Merriam puts it:

> . . . in practice this position was sharply challenged by the insistent demand for legislation and appropriation to serve various social and class purposes. Paradoxically, the general attitude was that of

hostility to governmental expansion as such or on any systematic theory, while in fact the demand for governmental activities went on at a rapid rate at the very urgent insistence of business, labor, agriculture, the professions and the general public. Each might be theoretically opposed to the extension of governmental functions, except in his particular instance. Thus high tariff was not inconsistent with the doctrine of laissez faire or prohibition with the idea of a minimum of government. And this after all was not inconsistent with the prevailing attitude of the time, which was that we had no theory but were essentially a practical people.

At the same time the federal functions spread, there has been an enlargement of the power and place of the expert. In 1896 there were 3,629 professional or scientific employees of the federal government. This was 2 per cent of the total employees. By 1931 this number had increased to 33,779, or 5.7 per cent of the total. The New Deal multiplied the number of experts, and the war has again multiplied that number. The people who prepared and those who adopted the Constitution in 1787 never dreamed of these experts or of the number of federal employees in other categories. "The number of individuals employed under the Constitution of the United States will be much smaller than the number employed under the particular States," Madison wrote in *The Federalist*. Today the employees of all the states are less in number than the civil employees under the Constitution of the United States.

The entry of specialists in great numbers into government is not solely in the capacity of service agencies for the people—such as agricultural experiment stations, services to advise exporters and importers, and social security. The government also employs specialists so that in dealing with technical problems it shall have as much knowledge in the particular field as is possessed by industry, commerce, labor, the universities, the medical profession and other technicians and the employers of those technicians.

Thousands of government specialists are engaged, on the other hand, in helping people to learn better ways of doing things. This is especially the case with the Department of Agriculture, which gives instruction to farmers in the most up-to-date scientific findings as to crops, fertilizers and plowing; advises their wives on nutrition and canning; and encourages young people to select farming as an occupation. And these activities are carried out not alone in laboratories and Washington offices, but on the farms themselves.

It is not only in government that there has been a tendency towards concentration and the multiplication of specialists. Nor is it only in the political realm that the authority has become the companion of economic power or the technician the nerve center of the enterprise. We have all known that the same development began in industrial life before it did in political. It has spread to the field of labor. The formula of concentration and the expert has been present for decades in transportation, the heavy industries and the automotive and chemical industries; it has spread in the retail trade and in the field of entertainment and refreshment and to some extent to textiles and much of our nationally advertised industry. It is a formula familiar to the older labor organizations and in its dynamic form is the core of the C.I.O. The walking delegate, the organizer, the labor educator, the labor economist—these are all specialists employed by organizations tending to increase the range of their power and the volume of their treasuries.

What a wide gap lies between the second bassoon and the president of the American Federation of Musicians, between the widow and orphan who own stock or bonds of the Pennsylvania Railroad and its president or the chairman of its board, between the soaking-pit craneman and the high officialdom of Bethlehem Steel! How far apart from the farmers are consumers of milk and cotton goods and pork products! What distances of space and hierarchy extend from the black share cropper of Arkansas to the Supreme Court and the government bureaus in Washington! These gulfs are threats to democracy because they represent dehumanized relations. They tend to make impossible those loyalties and to devitalize those attachments which, as John Dewey says, "are bred only in the intimacy of an intercourse which is of necessity restricted in range." When you can drop in at the mayor's law office or have the justice of the peace cut your hair or greet them daily on the street, government is your neighbor, your partner. But when its officials are far away, they tend to become awesome and abstract, and government becomes a mysterious machine of which the citizen does not feel a part and which he feels impotent to affect.

Just as the gargantuan corporation and cartel which belie *laissez faire* would have shocked Adam Smith, so the reliance on the technician to make policy would have distressed

Benjamin Franklin (at least to the ejaculation of an epigram), and the emergence of the federal government as the arbiter of American economic life and social organization would have stunned Jefferson. For Smith was the spokesman of an industrial revolution against the paternalism of the mercantile system, and Franklin and Jefferson were rebels not only against that system but against political paternalism as well.

Will these concentrations of political and economic power, will this willingness of people to accept dictation from scientists nowadays as to what is good for them, transmute democracy into a new paternalism? Must they lead to a new phase of patronage, through state socialism, or through a plutocracy of big business, or through a "managerial revolution"? I believe not—not if we understand the relation of the technician to the public—not if we avail ourselves of the new instrumentalities of local self-government which have been emerging. The new paternalism is indeed ripe; but just as the green bud of the second cutting of alfalfa shows before the first has flowered, new shoots of democracy, of co-operative opportunities, are present.

Although our schools now train technicians from beauty culturists to biochemists, from pinking-machine operators to legal philosophers; although public and private enterprise have seated specialists at the right hand of their lords, the problem of the expert is not new. His relationship to the public is an age-old controversy. His threatening position with respect to the seizure of power is well known as a cause for anxiety on the part of those who have held power and those who have wished to disperse it. I speak now not only of the technicians in military matters or financial affairs or the natural sciences, but also of those technicians in the arts of propaganda and government who have exploited each technique on which they could lay their hands for the aggrandisement of themselves and their associates.

The matter of the selection of experts and of an audit of the manner in which they exercised their specialties troubled the Greeks as it does society today. It was argued that the physician should be responsible to physicians who alone could judge of his competence; that "the right to exercise the elective power, . . . as well as the power of scrutiny, is the function exclusively of those who are masters of the science." Nevertheless Aristotle found, as we would today, that there is a mistake in the argument "unless the character of the masses is absolutely slavish"; for "although individually they are worse judges than the experts, yet in their collective capacity they are better or at least as good, and partly because there are some subjects in which the artist himself is not the sole or best judge, namely all those subjects in which the results produced are criticized equally well by persons who are not masters of the art." So, he says, it is not only the builder who should criticize the house or the carpenter the helm, or the cook the dinner, but the householder who uses the house and the pilot who uses the helm and the company that eats the dinner who are in a better position to appraise the work.

The same principles are inherent in part in De Tocqueville's comment on nineteenth-century American democracy, that popular government is educative as no other form of political control is, and in the suggestion of John Dewey that "the man who wears the shoe knows best that it pinches, if the expert shoemaker is the best judge of how the trouble is to be remedied."

The public is the best judge of the expert's efforts because, if one accepts the thesis of democratic society, it is the satisfaction of individual needs which is an aim of social organization and a condition to the realization of self. What does it matter whether the tax expert believes that a sales tax is the only effective way of raising funds for government if the public feels deprived by the sales tax of the means to the satisfaction of its hunger or desire for entertainment? What does it matter whether the expert believes that a sales tax is theoretically a violation of some tax pattern he conceives to be sound if the public is convinced that a sales tax is the only sure way of winning a war or maintaining education or relief services or accomplishing some social purpose? It is not the pattern of the doctor of philosophy that must be satisfied, any more than it is the pills of the doctor of medicine which must be consumed in order not to waste them or so as to keep the level of the contents of all the bottles of medicine uniform.

The development of a people can be stunted by the paternalism of science as readily as by that of church or state. It is only the official who regards his office as one for public service, and the man of God who looks upon himself as of service in bringing comfort and salvation who help men develop—not the official or churchman who tries to exercise control. The same is true of the specialist. To the degree to which he can be of service he is useful. But to the degree to which he seeks to impose his expert opinion as a new tablet of commandments inscribed by the manmade lightning bolts of the laboratory, he is no better than the German king who, in refusing the imperial crown from a revolutionary assembly, said that if that crown "is to be given away, then it will be *I* and my equals who will give it"; or the priest of ancient Rome who determined the course of empire by his reading of the entrails of the sacrifice. Uncontrolled technicians can become equally paternalistic and equally obscurantist.

Therefore, they must be guided by the people whose needs are to be served. They must perform their tasks in accordance with a popular mandate. They must be controlled by popular debate, discussion and judgment. The most intricate and clever machine must be set for the job it is to do: the most wise and clever expert must have his appointed task laid out for him. He is not *deus ex machina*.

What the hypothesis is to the laboratory scientist, the program of ends sought in the social and political field is to the expert—except that he does not ordinarily set his own problem as the laboratory scientist does. But this is by no means all.

In his *Experimental Medicine*, Claude Bernard writes:

> The revolution which the experimental method has effected in the sciences is this: it has put a scientific criterion in the place of personal authority.
>
> The experimental method is characterized by being dependent only on itself, because it includes within itself its criterion,—experience. It recognizes no authority other than that of facts and is free from personal authority. When Descartes said that we must

trust only to evidence or to what is sufficiently proved, he meant that we must no longer defer to authority, as scholasticism did, but must rely only on facts firmly established by experience.

In his *fact finding* and *planning* capacity, the government expert must also divorce himself from an attitude of authoritative certainty and accept experience as the criterion of his findings and advice. His task is relatively clear if he does not permit his compensation to be the purchase price of his honesty or his emotional biases to blind him to disagreeable and unsettling findings. But in his capacity as *administrator*, the government (or industrial or educational or welfare) expert faces other problems which are less those of scientist and more those of technician and artist.

It is not enough for the expert as administrator that there shall be a program of ends and the pursuit of truth regardless of authority. As administrator he must be in a position to attain results through action; and that action must give satisfaction to the group and individual needs of people. It is these needs which set his task. The fact that individual needs vary requires that the administrator first meet the more common needs, and then the more differentiated ones, even at the cost at times of doing conflicting things or choosing between those interests which the government will serve and those which it will ignore.

If the administrator is on an emotional level which requires rewards and the security to be found in an alliance with the more powerful interests, he will attempt to satisfy the needs of those interests. If, however, he can find satisfaction in a job well done, he will attempt to meet the interests of others too. The more broadly the weapons of power are diffused, the simpler will be his task in this.*

The expert, then, is something of a scientist, something of an administrator or something of both. In any event, to the extent that he becomes a member of a specialized class he shuts himself off from that experience which is essential to an appreciation of the needs he is supposed to serve. "A class of experts," Dewey says, "is inevitably so removed from common interests as to become a class with private interests and private knowledge, which in social matters is not knowledge at all." Managerial control of industry or expert control of government would be oligarchic in the same sense that control by any special group is oligarchic. It would be paternalistic just as any control is paternalistic which is not based on the active participation of the greatest possible number of people. Changing the word used to describe the few in control from the term "royal court" or "investment bankers" or "Nazi," "Fascist" or "Communist Party" to the term "managers" or "experts" or "administrators" does not change the basic patterns of political experience, that when the few govern, they govern in the interests of the few.

Furthermore, under whatever titles they have operated, persons in power or possessing weapons of power have as a general thing feared loss of power and prestige, possession and security; and those excluded from power as a rule have wished to destroy power and the hated human sym-

---

* For a further discussion of the weapons of power and the political process see *Swords and Symbols: The Technique of Sovereignty*, by the author, Oxford, New York, 1939.

bols of that power. Such patterns deter a realization of the ideals of democracy because they are laden with conflict and are inhospitable to mutual respect for individual dignity and the satisfaction of individual needs. The recognition of human dignity and achievement of satisfactions increase as the participation in control by all the members of a commonwealth, or other unit, is developed. Such participation produces the security of self-reliance. However, recognition of human dignity and achievement of satisfactions wane as the fear and passion inevitable to competition and to power politics make of control the prize of the selfish, the ruthless, the insecure, the avaricious and restless.

Let it not be thought that because control by expert or administrator runs counter to democratic principles and impedes democratic development, it must follow that expert and administrator must, therefore, be kept impotent to act in every respect. Pharaoh knew better when he made the eunuch Potiphar captain of the guard. Nor need the decisions of expert and administrator in each instance be subjected to canvass in advance and their action halted pending a vote. The ship might sink, the plague be spread, the electric power go off or innocent bystanders be killed by riot while action waited on plebiscite. Moreover, men and women cannot afford to spare the time and energy required to pass upon the minutiae of administrative action. An example is to be found in the American system of popular election of every local official. This was found to be unworkable; it was an invitation to the political careerist to take possession of the machinery of government and exact a toll on the use of that machinery for the benefit of predatory groups. The trend has been to concentrate on a few officers, who are then held to greater accountability. To quote once again from Woodrow Wilson:

> Self-government does not consist in having a hand in everything, any more than housekeeping consists necessarily in cooking dinner with one's own hands. The cook must be trusted with a large discretion as to the management of the fires and the ovens.

In our political thinking we are still affected by the primitive forms of the Anglo-Saxon hundreds and the New England town meeting. These are still relevant concepts for congregational or labor-union meetings; but the multiplication of technological knowledge and accomplishment and the millions of voting units concerned in an act of Congress or Parliament make the application of the town-meeting principle archaic today where either special knowledge or great masses of people are involved.

In consequence, we must look further than intimacy of contact with neighbors for control of the administrator and expert. We must seek something more than constitutional forms of checks and balances to counteract the tendency of the executive to absorb power. For, as William Seagle says in *The Quest for Law:*

> In all times the executive has been the primary state power. Indeed, it is the state power itself,* and

---

* This is the result of the common psychological identification of power with the father-figure, and where he is absent we frequently complete this identification by the creation of a new father-figure. Thus the great dictatorships of the last one hundred and fifty years have come to nations that have within a few months or years witnessed the defeat and humiliation of their established father-figures. Napoleon was substi-

for this very reason it is difficult to curb, despite all the recurrent attempts to subject it to control, to bring it within metes and bounds, to enmesh it in the chains of law.

New and vigorous means of popular control are necessary to delimit the metes and bounds of the vigorous new instruments of administration, those administrative boards or tribunals whose experts speak in the tongues of the sciences, and who preach to the public of quasi-mystical rules of social science, expert-made and with plus and minus figures thrown in for good measure.

Let it not be assumed that administrators are always aggressive or that the expert's expression of power is always affirmative. The instances of aggression and of positive action which interfere with popular needs and restrain the development of individuals are few and scattered compared to the negative occasions. Young people can be as gravely set back and held in adolescence by a parental "No" or lack of interest as by being told severely and superiorly, "You must." Except in revolutionary or quasi-revolutionary moments administration tends to the negative rather than to action. Cecil Thomas Carr stresses this point in his discussion of bureaucracy in *Concerning English Administrative Law:*

> To John Stuart Mill, who was emphatic that skilled and trained administrators were wanted for the government, the most fatal vice of bureaucrats

---

tuted for Louis XVI, Louis Napoleon for Louis Philippe, Mussolini for the humbled House of Savoy, Lenin and Stalin for the Czar and Hitler for the Kaiser.

was routine. . . . Something can perhaps be done to lever officials out of their grooves by transferring them to other duties from time to time. These plants are the better for periodical repotting. Mr. Harold Laski has elaborated Mill's indictment. When the civil servant attains seniority, he says, he becomes habituated to a routine of thought which deprecates innovation. . . . Any large-scale innovation is "ably and pertinaciously resisted" from within the civil service, which is "very nearly the perfect instrument for the negative state." And that, says Mr. Laski, is what a reforming President of the United States who abolished the patronage system would have to look out for.

We must again return to Wilson for a clear statement of principle and the theoretical answer to the apparent paradox of efficient administration and effective popular control. Of the study of administration he tells us:

> To be efficient it must discover the simplest arrangements by which *responsibility can be unmistakably fixed upon officials;** the best way of dividing authority without hampering it, and responsibility without obscuring it.

As to the part of the public:

> The right answer seems to be, that public opinion shall play the part of *authoritative critic.**

And finally:

---

* Italics mine.

Most important to be observed is the truth already so much and so fortunately insisted upon by our civil-service reformers; namely, that administration lies outside the proper sphere of *politics*. Administrative questions are not political questions. *Although politics sets the tasks for administration, it should not be suffered to manipulate its offices.**

Carr illuminates this point with a touch of political sagacity by suggesting:

> Political heads of departments in England might well claim it to be their function to tell the permanent officials how much the country will stand.

In summary, then, political action determines the field in which administration and expertness are to act, the ends which they are to pursue; the official responsibility for fulfilling the mandate of the people must be unmistakably fixed; and the public must remain the final critical authority—or, as Aristotle put it, the better judge of the dinner than the cook.

So much for the theory. But how shall it be implemented? How shall the babble of voices, the confusion of popular tongues, be clarified to set tasks and speak with critical authority in a world threatened by tyrannous experts in administration?

Let us review what has already been said. We have seen that the administrator tends to absorb power to himself, and that a group of experts can become an oligarchy just as can any other group which gains control of a major part of

---

* Italics mine.

the weapons of sovereignty. But strict control of the administrator, close limitation of the expert, in government or any other field, defeats the purpose of expertness, which must have scope for experiment and investigation. Neither an entry clerk nor a plant pathologist nor the engineer of a power project can do his job well to the kibitzing of every barber, every typist, every lawyer or every publicity agent, although he must be responsible to all of them as members of democratic society.

Administrators, and through them other experts, must be controlled, not by interference in technical detail, but by means of public canvassing of their acts and public criticism of their deviations from what the public believes will meet its needs. They must be controlled through expression by the public of its aims and the needs which it requires to be satisfied. These will frequently be diverse and conflicting; but in a democracy the administrator will assume this to be the case and attempt to give to each interest according to the variety of its needs and to reconcile conflicting interests as far as possible. He will discover that the broader the base of popular control—that is, the greater the diffusion of sovereign weapons of force, wealth and propaganda—the less critical will be the conflicts.

We have also noticed that, as the social, economic and technological problems become more complex and the political unit becomes numerically larger, the contact between the individual member of the public and the responsible administrator becomes more tenuous. How, then, can individuals set forth the problems for the administrator and technician to meet? How can they canvass the acts of the experts, how perform the function of authoritative critics?

The answer may be found in new democratic forms that have sprouted in the shadow of the mammoths. With that adaptability which living forms possess and that power of adjustment which healthy organisms evidence, the psychological drive toward equality and recognition has found democratic expression. The union of workers has been a response to the paternalism of the employer who considered himself alone capable of determining wages and working conditions and the terms of hire and fire. The consumer co-operative and the farm co-operative have been voices raised against the paternalism of commerce, which presumed to determine price and quality and variety of merchandise in its own interest. The functional Industry Committee and farm committee have superseded the old forms of government in vital fields by standing between communities of interest and the paternalistic threat of centralized government.

Much of the federal government's business is transacted by local boards and committees under the authority of federal law. During the second, as in the first World War, the draft has been administered largely through local draft boards. Civilian defense is conducted by state and local civilian defense councils and local civil authorities, although federal authorities may set the pattern. Under the Wages and Hours Act it is committees of employers and employees in the several industries who set standards.

The greatest program of local management, however, is under the Department of Agriculture. It involves county and state committees elected by farmers, and in some instances set up after a referendum of farmers, to administer the crop adjustment program, rural electrification, control of grazing, soil conservation, contour farming and the like. Here the national government sets the program (in vital instances on referendum) and the pattern of administration and provides the technicians, sometimes in collaboration with states; but local authorities locally selected do the work of administration.

Similarly, the federal subventions to vocational education are granted to the states to be administered by locally chosen school boards under standards set by the technicians of state educational departments.

These are functional local authorities. Except for school boards, many of them are still extraordinary rather than common institutions, but they represent the beginnings of new instrumentalities of government within hailing distance of the people concerned with the particular function of government to be served. If it is true, as Sir Frederick Pollock has said, that "extraordinary jurisdictions succeed by becoming ordinary," then we may expect to see the march of federal authority accompanied by the creation of new strong points of democratic local participation.

The short-lived wonder, NRA, introduced to American businessmen the concept that guild chivalry was not dead. They learned that, in spite of the threat of anti-trust laws and the even more imminent threat of destruction at the hands of industrial enterprise too large to be seriously hampered by anti-trust laws, men might lay down rules of fair practice in their field and speak as a group directly to the government, not merely as individuals or loose trade association through the mediation of lobbyists and lawyers. NRA passed out, but it may be expected that its pattern will be revived in the interest of survival—and also in the interest of minimizing bureaucracy under even a limited form of planned economy. Bureaucracy may adopt more drastic rules for the control of business than would interested parties. But businessmen are more likely to enforce their own rules made to implement government policy than those made by public officials. Certainly the guild merchants did a better job of it than most government bureaus have. And when the courts of England took jurisdiction over commercial law, they found it more feasible to incorporate those customs of merchants known as "the law merchant" than to stretch the common law rules derived from feudal society. Businessmen are hardly popular today. But their sins cannot be the subject of retributive justice by crushing them with the heavy hand of government —that is, not unless some sort of communism is to be introduced and private enterprise abolished.

One of the most serious sins of the business world has been its patronizing of its employees, its domination of the labor market. But again, to substitute for this form of paternalism that of the labor czar is change but not progress, is variation without growth. There is no difference insofar as the right to work is concerned or the security of living between the boss and the labor leader who arbitrarily says that a man shall or shall not work on a particular job—or any job at all. Nor is there in substance any difference between the corporation which hires "private police" to break the heads of workers who threaten its authority by organizing or striking and the labor leader who uses thugs to batter the heads of union members who threaten his authority by organizing opposition within the union or by demanding an accounting on the floor of the union convention.

This is only a substitution of one arbitrary paternalism for another.

The essence of unionism is that it offers brotherhood rather than paternalism; that through fraternity its members will gain security and, out of that security of equals, face the would be dictators of industry or government as their equals. Of course, such organization lends itself to gangsterism; but have we not frequently witnessed other institutions, including perverted religion, indulge in gangsterism? Thus it was not the tyranny of Calvin in Geneva but the democratic Calvinism of the Scotch and English countryside that broke the back of English monarchical power.

A democratically conducted labor union is a co-operative enterprise essential to the maintenance of democratic society. It is a functional substitute for the lost neighborliness of urban communities and the diminishing vitality of the older forms of local government. It offers the opportunity for personal recognition on a more adult, a less escapist basis than fraternal groups. It is also the school for training men and women in the art of canvassing the acts of their elected administrators and staffs of experts and also in the methods of setting forth the ends which they expect those administrators and experts to pursue. However, to have such values for democracy, the mechanics of democratic unionism must be assured even, if necessary, by government guaranty of the rights of individual members to express their grievances, freedom from arbitrary dismissal, and a public accounting as to the use of union funds. For if the union official can with impunity suppress all complaints, dismiss members without notice and a hearing, or handle the workers' funds as he alone sees fit, the union is not a democratic institution, but an estate of the official. A parallel is to be found in the legal rights of stockholders which rarely hamper legitimate activity by corporate management, but which in most instances avoid the freezing out of minorities. The protection of labor-union minorities is even more essential, for today the worker and his organization are more necessary to the preservation of democratic forms and the spread of democratic practice than is the corporation. The proof of the pudding is to be found in the fact that the fascist nations have continued corporations, which did not threaten the corporative state, and destroyed the independent labor organizations, which were a threat.

If unions are to achieve the fulfillment of their possibilities as democratic institutions, or if they are to be the mature expression of men and women insofar as concerns earning a living, then they must have greater voice in the management of industry. At the very least, management should take the workers into their confidence to explain the major problems of the concern and the effectiveness of the plant and its several divisions. It should set up some standards of effectiveness which the worker can understand, other than the piece-work standard, and in which he feels that he has an interest. Men like to feel the success of the enterprise of which they are part. That is a wholesome form of identification and creative collaboration. Naturally, they also want to succeed by advancing themselves financially and in power; that is the test of success to which they have been educated by the business world. But they will accept limitations on their personal success stories better—that is, with less sense of failure and grievance—if they are treated as adults, if someone in authority makes a point of clarifying to them their own relationship to the end result of the enterprise. Cooke and Murray say in their stimulating *Organized Labor and Production:*

> At times it almost seems as if there was a studied effort to keep those responsible for some subdivision of the total effort from knowing how results compare with the results being obtained elsewhere in the same establishment.

Such an attitude is not compatible with obtaining the best efforts from workers. It is a carryover of an archaic pattern of authoritarianism, which assumes that management must represent capital alone. It is irrelevant in the logic of society which makes collective bargaining public policy. "Just forget that you have any authority and we will get ahead with our task," Cooke and Murray quote Quartermaster General Robert E. Wood (now chairman of the board of Sears, Roebuck and Company) as saying to his staff in the first World War. By more of such a cooperative attitude and less of the attitude of competition and aggression, much of the tension could be removed from employer-labor relations. And it is important not only to employers and workers, but to all of the people, that this tension be relieved, not so much in the interests of greater production and more continuous employment as because it is a constant threat to political and social stability.

While someone or some group must have authority to make final decisions, it is an admission of insecurity on the part of authority to assume that it is exempt from collaboration in the planning stages and free of responsibility to give reasons for decisions. Industry cannot indefinitely remain authoritarian in a democratic society. In the long run organized labor will assume greater responsibility in industrial planning and control. It must assume such responsibility as the alternative to state control with the threat of totalitarian state capitalism which that involves. This issue has been well expressed by Golden and Ruttenberg in *The Dynamics of Industrial Democracy*, as follows:

> The philosophy underlying Philip Murray's Industry Council program is intrinsically democratic. It is the philosophy . . . that the principal groups in our free society should get together to solve their mutually dependent problems instead of either neglecting them or leaving them to a centrally constituted governmental bureaucracy to try and solve. During the nineteen thirties we became disillusioned by the opposite philosophy. It is basically impractical, since it is predicated upon the idea of referring unsolved economic and social problems to someone else. Instead of organized labor and management, in co-operation with government, getting together to solve their mutual problems they turn them over to Congress, then let Congress pass legislation and thereby turn them over to an administrative agency.

This "running-to-the-government" trend is not the way to develop a self-reliant democracy. Even the most democratic government acting as arbitrator—with its inherent threat of force—is only a substitute, an *ersatz* provision for the democracy of co-operative effort.

Another democratic answer to the mammoths of centralized government and industry and to the decline of local government lies in the consumer and producer co-operatives. The vital democratic feature of both unions and co-operatives is not so much the equality which their members possess in voting and privileges of membership as in the fact that by these instruments men have undertaken to make themselves masters of their own fate as workers and consumers. That is, of course, why totalitarian states have destroyed co-operatives or, as in the Soviet Union, made them agencies of the state.

It is less than a hundred years since the twenty-eight impoverished mill workers of Rochdale opened their basement-room grocery store on a capital of $140. By 1934 seven million Britishers representing one-half the families of the kingdom were co-operative members. One-twelfth of the country's retail trade was done by the co-operatives. The wholesale society had 139 factories. It was the greatest single producer of flour, shoes and soap in England. The co-operative's banking department did a business equal to that of the fourth largest bank in the country.

Before the war, in Denmark the dairy co-operative was patronized by 192,000 out of 206,000 farmers and handled almost half of the butter and 90 per cent of the milk produced. The co-operatives did the major part of the Danish agricultural export business. They reversed the trend toward tenant farming so that in 1935 at least 97 per cent of the farmers owned their land. In the United States only 58 per cent farmed their own farms.

In Sweden the co-operatives were trust busters. They defeated the margarine cartel and broke the high prices of sugar, soap, flour, galoshes and light bulbs, among other things.

Less spectacularly in other lands the co-operative movement spread on every continent. It is the backbone of the economy of New Zealand and since the Japanese invasion, of the fugitive industry of China.

In spite of chain-store competition in the United States, there were more than 2,000 consumer co-operative societies here in 1940, with more than a million members (as against 704,000 in 1935) and a business turnover of $200,000,000. Together with producer co-operatives, the turnover was almost $600,000,000, and the membership two millions.

Not alone have co-operatives brought economic benefits to their members; they have also introduced a unit of neighborliness, experience in self-rule and satisfaction in management of which the members felt deprived by aggressive local politicians and the declining vitality of local governments. And while co-operatives are compatible with capitalism in that both involve free enterprise, they invert the functions of capital by making it serve the consumer instead of subjecting the consumer to the dedication of capital to profits.

Moreover, the very fact that ownership has turned over the operation of large sections of industry and commerce to experts, has made it clear that success in business does not depend on the man with the dollar giving his personal service to the operation. Consequently, if salaried employees can run power plants for the utility companies, they can run them for the Tennessee Valley Authority or a village; and if salaried employees can conduct chain stores and gas stations, they can conduct co-operative retail stores and gas services. Thus in other fields men are learning what lawyers have known for centuries, that the man who pays the bill can acquire the expert's skill.

If the fundamentals of a democratic society are to be secure, then, in the face of the mammoths and their experts, it must be through the extension of the new local and co-operative formulae in the political and consumer fields and in productive and industrial life. Except in rare instances, one cannot look to political "leaders" for leadership in this extension. The office-holder will find a challenge to his authority in the newer political agencies. The old county agent, for example, is likely to resent the soil conservation expert, though he comes as the result of a vote by the farmers of the conservation area. There will be little help from experts in politics in the development of democratic forms, because, as Governor Alfred E. Smith pointed out in *The Citizen and His Government*, it is these groups that stand in the way of reform.

> . . . the dominant political groups of every party and every locality stand firmly in the way of reform. This is very easy to understand. These groups live on the patronage of town and county government. The taxpayers' money paid in salaries to the political henchmen serves to keep the organization together. Any attempt at reformation is still bound to meet with the vigorous opposition of these selfish people.

After all, politicians are power mongers in their own rite, and it is therefore not to be expected that many of them will possess sufficient emotional security to support those co-operative enterprises of workers and consumers which would make government and its officialdom less important. Yet this is what would occur if labor were afforded greater responsibility in the conduct of industry and if co-operatives were sufficiently widespread to constitute yardsticks of commercial practice. Through their individual development and their assumption of group responsibility —as the result of participation in the activities of their unions and their co-operatives—the members would be better trained to set the tasks and judge the results of their government administrators and experts. It could scarcely be expected that this would appeal to men with an urge to personal power or private gain.

It is not only the negativeness of politicians which impedes the development of those democratic processes which will relieve men and women from the paternalism of industrial management and the profit-inspired market. Today there is the equal threat of the Marxian fallacy that the inequalities of the world can be removed by the triumph of the proletariat in a class struggle which must end in public ownership (and of course management) of the means of production. The end result of state capitalism through its concentration of power in the experts of administration is a barrier to equality and to the recognition of the dignity of the individual. It entrenches the administrators as oligarchs because it gives them control, not only of the sovereign weapon of physical force, but also of economic power and inevitably also of propaganda. And over years these are more effective weapons than force. This is expressed in one clear sentence by Rudolf von Ihering:

"Coercion is effective only so long as the whip is in sight; remuneration works continually."

There is less danger to the individual and his integrity as a human being, and therefore to democratic society, in a capitalist economy balanced by active participation in industrial management by organized labor and by the active self-help of organized consumers, than there is in state capitalism. Furthermore, the machinery of government cannot be controlled by private industry where labor and consumer organizations and organizations of small producers, such as farm co-operatives, are active. This has been illustrated by the prewar experience of the Scandinavian nations.

It is hard for many people to realize this because they see only the predatory history of the drive for profit making and cannot recognize their own power as dynamic forces in a system of free enterprise through the potency of organized labor and consumers. Furthermore, men are so accustomed to being the victims of marauding and enslavement by those in power that they lack the self-confidence to realize that in the labor union and the co-operative they possess red meat to make of themselves men and the equals of any man. It is only as they acquire this confidence that they will meet aggression in a manner that will assure them equality. Without this confidence, reform and revolution will be the repetition of the old story of substituting one paternalistic situation for another.

So we see how in the last half-century expert and technician have assumed important places in government and industry. This has both brought about and been brought about by the complexity and technical development of government and industry; and it has been accompanied by concentration. This in turn has changed the relations of state and federal governments and led to the enfeeblement of traditional local institutions. Such developments as these would have dismayed the founders of democratic government and the fathers of *laissez faire*.

The working out of the logic of competition has brought chaotic results to industry. The increased financial powers of centralized governments and the emergence of new administrative instruments such as administrative boards or tribunals have resulted in the upset of the old balances between national government and local. These concentrations which we experience today have created a gap between the citizen and his government, the worker and his employer, such as was unknown to the medieval world with its neat organization of mutual loyalties and responsibilities.

Unless the relationship between government and citizen is to become a new and greater paternalism than anything we have known before—except perhaps the paternalism of the Axis powers and the Soviet Union—the position of the expert and of the administrative board must be clarified. The public must undertake to judge them and their results; it must be "authoritative critic"; it must set the tasks of experts and administrators and appraise their accomplishments. Otherwise we shall have an oligarchy of experts—particularly as the expert in government is entrusted with great powers.

Control by the people cannot become effective through reliance on a revival of old, faltering institutions. Popular control and the renaissance of local institutions must be accomplished through new functional institutions. In this category are such developments as county agricultural committees, labor unions and co-operatives both of producers and consumers. These represent co-operative efforts. They are based on attitudes of mutual respect and collaboration, not on aggression or subservience.

6

Wayward Nations

WHEN GIRLS AND BOYS are delinquent today—that is, when their conduct is such that their relationship to other people is in conflict with what society approves and their behavior is of a dissocial nature—we no longer treat them as wild beasts or as bewitched by devils or as hopeless outcasts. We do not feel satisfied to beat them into submission or to sit and pray for their recovery or to attempt to drive out the devil by the magic of words or to leave them to recover by themselves—if they do not get into more serious trouble before recovery. Modern penology demonstrates that a more scientific approach brings better results. So we study our delinquent. We find out what we can about his body, his mind and his emotions. We learn what we can concerning the environment in which he has been growing up, and we plan how we can turn him into a good citizen, a useful and social human being, an individual capable of finding satisfaction on a level of social rather than dissocial conduct. We do this by correcting, where we can, his physical defects and his major psychological conflicts. We teach him the tools of learning and of trade and attempt to make it possible for him to achieve economic security. We try to make him capable of acting under his own power and of assuming responsibility for his own acts, and we aim to avoid leaving him with an attitude of dependence on others for his good behavior. Then, having started him towards recovery, we do not immediately set him adrift to be all on his own, to play with pistols or join the corner gang once more. We place him on probation so that he will have supervision and guidance; so that there will be someone to go to when he feels defeated by his life.

Now let us consider two wayward nations, Germany and Japan. In discussing these nations in terms of the psychology of delinquency, I am well aware that there are dangers in the application of individual behavior problems to group behavior. I am also conscious of the truth expressed by Jawaharlal Nehru in his autobiography, where he says:

> As soon as one begins to think of the other side as a mass or a crowd, the human link seems to go. We forget that crowds also consist of individuals, of men and women and children, who love and hate and suffer.

We should remember, then, at all times that Germany and Japan are not abstractions but millions of human beings "who love and hate and suffer," and who vary each from another in many ways. We should bear in mind that as human beings they are not isolated, and their behavior is not that of isolated units independent of each other. Rather, the behavior of the German and Japanese nations is the direct result of the relations and attitudes of individual Germans and Japanese with and towards other Germans and Japanese as individuals and groups, and their relations with and attitudes towards other nations and their peoples. There is no identity between the people who live and work, who love and hate and suffer along Main Street; they have not all the same attitudes; they do not all act in the same way; and yet Main Street is what it is because of the individual relationships toward family and neighbors and competitors and the ancestors who laid the cornerstones and the people who live across the tracks. For all their differences, they exhibit definable group tendencies and behavior, they have certain ends and ideals in common. As it is with Main Streeters, so it is with Germans and Japanese.

The conduct of the wayward nations and their attitudes towards other lands are a composite of the behavior and attitudes of millions of Germans and Japanese, and especially of the behavior and attitudes of those groups that possess a preponderance of the weapons of sovereignty, who through the possession of economic and propagandistic power can achieve the power of physical force, or at least that reputation for it which we call prestige. The behavior and attitudes of these nations parallel those of gangster groups. This is particularly true of those who dominate these nations. They have used gangster methods and have been moved by gangster psychology. They have been dissocial units in the community of nations; they are power-craving political organisms. This is not to say that all or even most Germans or Japanese are gangsters or dissocial or power-craving.

Thomas Mann, who could write *Tonio Kröger* and *Joseph in Egypt*; Arnold Zweig, who could create out of the first World War a *Sergeant Grischa*; Erich Remarque, who could produce *All Quiet On The Western Front*; Albert Einstein, who could conceive of the whole universe in terms of relativity; and millions of unknown and lesser Manns, Zweigs, Remarques and Einsteins are neither gangsters nor dissocial nor power-craving. They are descendants of the tradition of Goethe and Schiller, of Lessing and Heine. They have been a social motif in German life, a conscience, a theme of brotherly love and of democratic longing in the German people.

Nor must we forget that among the men and women and children of Japan who love and hate and suffer there are not only those people nurtured in the traditions of the war-lusting *Samurai* but also those humble people whose love of beauty and the ways of peace have created with meticulous care gardens wherever they have lived, and gentle people such as those whose hospitality was described by Anne Lindbergh in *North to the Orient*.

Yet time and again for centuries the blustering and brutal elements have taken control of German affairs and possession of the German imagination and have colored the life and the ideals of the Japanese people. It is as though the German and the Japanese peoples, like wayward youngsters, were seized by a compulsion to destroy and dominate, a compulsion that neither a sense of guilt nor a drive towards brotherly love could divert or dissuade. As in the case of the delinquent child, there is a history of feelings of inferiority, of melancholic depressions alternating with bluster, of Wagners and Nietzsches and Fichtes, of Schopenhauers and *Sturm und Drang*—a history of insecurity and retreat punctuated by the harsh regimen of *bushido*.

The very history of the German people is unique in such elements. When the Roman Empire fell before the barbarian invasions, it fell to untutored hordes unstabilized by tradition or a developed culture and insecure in its semi-nomadic economy. And these hordes were largely German. They were at a cultural and economic level inferior to that of Rome, and because of these deficiencies were unable to create a stabilized society out of events which were revolutionary. They had triumph without achieving victory, without possessing the social and political maturity which would have enabled them to get satisfaction out of the equalitarian possibilities at hand. They could not help but feel ashamed of this cultural immaturity in the face of Roman civilization and Christian idealism. Attila the Hun halted at the appeal of the Pope and spared the city. The German tribes entered and sacked it, and like the man whose guilt and need of punishment bring him again to the scene of his crime, they repeated their offense throughout the centuries.

At the time the Roman era ended, the German tribes east of the Rhine had scarcely been touched by Roman rule or by the Church of Rome. Gaul had had five hundred years' more contact with the imperial civilization. Open to attack from the east and the west, the tribes beyond the Rhine lacked the insular security of the Anglo-Saxons; and, as tribal lands became more static and nomadic habits were succeeded by an agricultural economy, the Germans settled down to an uncertain living, to the insecurities of unprotected fields and forests, uncertain crops and unwritten tribal culture. There was no national unity, no legal system that embraced them all as the system of Rome had included in its embrace the Roman Empire. The tribal law covered each member of every tribe no matter where he might be geographically established or among what other group he was living. But there was no German law for all.

When it became possible to assert power once more on a large scale, it was not the east Germans but the Frankish people who took over in the name of Empire. It was Charlemagne who was recognized by the Bishop of Rome, who was invincible, who created a court and schools and revived some of the glory that had been Rome's. Latin culture and the remnants of its customs and institutions afforded a centralizing influence and understanding which was necessary to permit the Empire to develop in France. The Germans had not yet fully evolved from tribal life or accepted the social order and responsibilities of feudalism.

A century and a half later, the Saxons who, as heathens, had been overcome by Charlemagne produced the Ottonian line of Kings and Holy Roman Emperors culminating in Henry IV. The great drama over the right of investiture, the struggle between emperor and pope over the power to select bishops, came to a climax between Henry and Hildebrand, Pope Gregory VII. (It is interesting to note that this theme of state over church recurs again in German history in the doctrine of Luther, in the *Ich und Gott* of Kaiser Wilhelm II and in the policy of Hitler.) Henry defied the Pope and called upon him to relinquish the apostolic chair, whereupon Gregory excommunicated Henry. This destroyed the unity of the German church and caused rebellion among the German princes.

Then Henry took the historic journey to Canossa. A penitent, he humbled himself before the Pope until his assertions of repentance won him absolution and the ban was lifted. Thus, almost nine hundred years ago the symbol of German power and unity was humbled. The bad boy bowed the knee to gain forgiveness and avoid punishment. The father-figure of the land was humiliated in the sight of all the children. And what followed? Henry broke his promise of safe conduct of the Pope to Augsburg. He renewed the investiture struggle. He invaded the lands of the Pope, he set up an anti Pope and drove Gregory into exile. Canossa was in the spirit of Versailles. It was a verbal triumph only. There was no lesson learned to modify behavior. All that happened was that the defeated said in effect: "You've broken me this time, but wait. My chance will come."

Not long after Henry, the Empire collapsed again into territorial states. When Martin Luther set forth his thesis, empire was a theory, not a fact. He led the way from political and spiritual domination by the Church of Rome, but he left the authority of the state as it was. It was only clerical authoritarianism he rejected; civil authority he accepted. This was not true of Calvinism. There was a leaven of reform in that Protestantism which led through the democratic presbytery to the Cromwellian Revolution and through the Huguenots to the French Revolution.

The Thirty Years' War left Germany a shambles, impoverished in population and economy, broken politically. That national unity which was developing in France and England was deferred for centuries in Germany.

Insecure and distrustful, Prussia commenced at last to

feel a stirring in its sinews, and under the dynasty of the Great Elector and Frederick William I and Frederick the Great became a power on the European continent. Bourbon France was the model; French words were Germanized and Voltaire was court jester. The principle upon which this development was based was expressed by the Great Elector in these words: "Alliances may be all very well, but power of your own is better." Friendship, brotherhood, trust and co-operation may be all very well for the secure; but the insecure, the humiliated, must work on the assumption that one mustn't trust anyone else. This is typical delinquent psychology.

For all the great triumphs of Prussia, the post-revolutionary armies of Napoleon destroyed Prussian power again at Jena and Valmy. More than power was destroyed, however. Pride and self-respect were crushed. Tyranny and exploitation were instituted under the fanciful title of "Liberty, Equality and Fraternity." Benjamin Constant in his contemporary study of Napoleonism wrote:

> In the past, the representatives of a conquered people had to crawl on their knees before their conquerors; today it is the conscience of man which must be prostrated.

Germany was one of the conquered peoples whose conscience was prostrated. Humbled by the French Emperor, it learned a technique by which with vengeance it could humiliate and tyrannize over other conquered peoples. It learned, too, that words "aren't always what they seem."

So Germany entered the nineteenth century beaten, dispersed, intellectually confused, in need of security and authority. Emmanuel Kant writes of man whose ends are shaped by a categorical imperative, and thus makes it almost impossible for Germans bred in his philosophy to accept the relativity of ends or the pragmatic attitude of democracy. Heine, eager to be accepted as German and yet unable himself blindly to accept Germany, writes:

> It is the greatest merit of Christianity to have assuaged the joy of the German in brutal bellicosity, but it has not been able to eradicate that joy completely, and when, one day, the Cross of Christ is broken, the savagery of the old warriors, the wild Berserker wrath, will break forth anew in all the barbaric fury of which our Nordic poets tell in song and saga. . . . Thor will leap forth, brandishing his mighty hammer, to break the Gothic cathedrals. . . . Do not laugh at my advice—the advice of a dreamer who warns you against the disciples of Kant and Fichte, and the pantheist philosophers. Do not sneer at one who foretells the same revolution in the world of action which has been accomplished in the world of thought. Thought precedes action as sure as lightning precedes thunder. German thunder is admittedly German: it is not very agile, and it rumbles a bit slowly: but it will come one day, and, when you hear an explosion such as has never yet occurred in the history of the world, then you will know that it is German thunder. . . .

Nietzsche and others are concerned with what they deemed the cultural backwardness of Germany. There is much talk of the German spirit in the past and in the future; there is little readiness to accept themselves for what they are. They romanticize as young girls and boys do, indulging in fantacies of infancy and of what they would do when they grew up. They revel in tales of Wotan and Siegfried and dream of supermen. Hegel and Marx, glorifying struggle, the one mapping the "perfect Prussian state," the other proclaiming the need for a "dictatorship of the proletariat," round out the picture. Here were dreams of the insecure, of those whom life had defeated, dreams of strength, force, struggle; nothing of the rights of man, of natural rights, no pragmatic concept of law and government such as we find in Locke and Austin.

Twenty years ago Beatrice Hinkle commented:

> If our world had been one in which philosophy, science and poetry were held in equal regard with trade, commerce and machinery, Germany might have continued to use her own functions in the realm for which they are fitted and have found her path to power along lines where her supremacy could hold unchallenged. Then the history of the world would have been differently written.

This passage is at least suggestive of the part that ends and values may have in stimulating national political drives.

With Bismarck and the First Reich, Germany emerged from its spiritual depression and commenced a manic half-century of bluster and braggadocio. There was once more an Emperor and a powerful paternalistic state to give promise of security and to issue categorical imperatives. There were the Von Moltkes and Bernhardis and the Iron

Chancellor himself to exalt "blood and iron." With the Wagnerian Valhalla of a pagan past as a point of departure, the Reich was to ignore the humiliations of centuries and repress all individual yearnings in the interest of what Hegel had described as the "common will" expressed in the state. It was not the individual who was important, but rather the family group presided over by a stern and powerful father—that is, the Reich dominated by the Kaiser in spite of parliamentary forms. For the parliamentarianism of the Reich was hamstrung by the powers vested in the Kaiser and in the rulers of the local states.

The reference made to the position of the German father in the German family is not a slight matter. It is the foundation of the German attitude toward authority and the apparent insecurity of adult Germans without a strong political father-figure; it is at the basis of their ready acceptance of the *Verboten*, of state totemism and taboo. Here, too, is the seed pod of sadism and destruction which have been so prominent in recent years. The German father has dominated the German family in a manner which it is difficult for Americans or Englishmen or Frenchmen or Russians to realize. It is no accident, but an essential characteristic of the German spirit in search of security, that Germans do not talk of a mother country, but of a *Vaterland*.

This has given rise to the suggestion that Germany as a nation is in conflict, in that it is trying to live out a masculine role when instinctively it has feminine reactions to masculine symbols. Hitler himself has emphasized this in *Mein Kampf*, where he describes the masses in terms of a woman:

> Like a woman whose feelings are determined less by abstract reason than by a kind of indefinable, emotional longing for fulfilling strength, and who, therefore, prefers to bow to the strong than to command the weak, the masses prefer him who comes to them as a master to him who comes to them with an appeal, and feel inwardly more satisfied by a doctrine which tolerates no rival than by liberal freedom. With the latter it knows very little what to do, and even derives a sense of neglect from it.

After reading this quotation, it is reasonable to suppose that the German absorption in guns and power is due in part to the unusually large proportion of German men of abnormal sexual behavior acting under an inner compulsion to prove that they are masculine, to emulate the dominating fathers of their youth.

Whatever the validity of the suggestion of confusion of roles may be, it is certain that the position of the father-figure in German social organization has afforded a basis for the paternalism of Hitler and his predecessors who controlled the Prussian state. It is also undeniable that Germany, unable to find satisfaction in its genius for production and scientific inventiveness, felt compelled to enter the lists of international competition. It did not just try to sell its surplus goods abroad, it tried to *overtake* Great Britain in trade, in colonial expansion and in armaments. Its competitive spirit prior to the first World War was intermeshed with its search for power and recognition of its prestige. Bismarck utilized the wars against Austria and the Empire of Napoleon III as means of creating a unified world power out of the numerous feeble German states.

The adolescent boy, uncertain of his strength and masculinity, has to prove his growth by distributing black eyes and carrying a chip on his shoulder. Kaiser Wilhelm II was forever carrying a chip on his shoulder, building his navy and threatening from the Philippines to North Africa.

The social security program initiated by Bismarck was the foremost paternalistic move of modern times. While the political rationalization ascribed to Bismarck for this program was a countermove against the threat of socialism, it fell in with the German psychological attitude toward paternalism.

So that there be no misunderstanding, I hasten to point out that social security need not be and has not always been paternalistic. Social insurance was introduced in Great Britain by the Asquith government after a triumph of Liberalism over Tory concepts of government. Similar programs have been introduced in Australia and New Zealand through democratic movements and the participation of labor parties. The co-operative housing ventures in Austria before Hitler absorbed that country were definitely democratic, as were the social programs in the Scandinavian lands. The New Deal was the result of a popular demand that working men and women be assured protection against the paternalism implicit in the arbitrary system of hire and fire by private industry.

Social security can, then, be a step in democratic progress, a means for securing equality. But this was not the case in Germany. There social insurance was like the Roman bread and circuses, the British dole and the early days of the American Works Progress Administration: it was so much candy to quiet baby.

Following the humiliation by the Treaty of Versailles, the German people entered a cycle of melancholy. It was a nation in debt and economic collapse, suffering from rickets and unacknowledged guilt. As a political body Germany had suffered mayhem through the loss of its colonies and Alsace Lorraine. Inflation was a similar injury to the middle class. France, knocking repeatedly at the door, reparations bill in hand, and surrounding Germany with bayonets-in-alliance, was a continuous threat of a new blockade and of a repetition of years of malnutrition. All this had its effect on German psychology.

A psychologically healthier nation, you may say, might have accepted punishment for guilt without the compulsion to rebel or to seek for repeated punishment. A more mature nation might have found satisfaction in its great constructive and creative capacity. It would have accepted peace and work. But the same might be said of wayward children: if they were healthier minded or emotionally more mature, they would not get into trouble, they would not shoplift or throw stones through windows or light fires in baby carriages or molest little girls. However, they do do these things. So the treatment of wayward children—and wayward nations—necessitates special attention.

It is also possible that if Germany had experienced a genuinely popular revolution at the end of the first World War the depth of its psychological depression would not have been so great. For revolutions are a part of the growing-up process of groups or classes of people, as is the assumption of independence and responsibility by adolescents. Through revolution they declare freedom from the prevailing paternalism. If they are prepared to assume maturity, some strong democratic system will be evolved. If not, they may flounder among democratic forms while hoping for a new paternalism, as happened in Germany; or they may select a substitute father-figure promptly, as the Russian people substituted Lenin and Stalin for the "Little Father" who wore the crown of the Romanoffs.

However, the Spartacist Revolution inspired by Liebknecht and Rosa Luxemburg was crushed, and the more conservative socialists took hold of affairs and imagined for a time that they controlled the life and policy of the German people. Walter Rathenau, one of the great industrialists and certainly one of the great statesmen and political writers of the period, commented on the situation in these words:

> The World Revolution began with the outbreak of the World War. Its unconscious but real and practical object was the substitution of a capitalist middle class for the feudal nobility as rulers in a plutocratic State governed on constitutional lines.

But the middle class was not there. It never took control in Germany as it did in Britain, France and the United States.

Unfortunately, inflation destroyed much of the middle class, but not the German *Junkers*, not the feudal nobility who, with the great industrialists and the newly enriched speculators and the old generals, crowded Ebert and the Weimar Republic. Germany, therefore, never has had the catharsis of a popular revolution, as have Britain, France and the American Colonies. When its middle-class revolution did take place, it was too late; the middle class washed out and left the great monopolies, the great landowners and the generals to nullify the democratic efforts of the labor unions.

The German spirit was confused; it was depressed irrespective of economic depression. It did not have those spiritual resources and that self-confidence essential to find satisfaction in united co-operative effort; it could find in fraternity no substitute for paternalism. It was humiliated and longed for approval; it was guilty and needed forgiveness or further punishment. The father-figure of the World War had become emasculated; he was an old man sawing wood in exile. The alternative offered by the left was a man of another country, another race, quasi-oriental. He was a threat to the barons of industry and land and the memory of Bismarck; and he was not of the same school as the *Reichswehr* with its tradition of Frederick the Great.

It was the old-line elements who first found a savior in Hitler, the demagogue, and revealed him to the people as the *Führer*. When finally he became patron of industry and army as well as of the common people, it was too late, for the lost and wandering ghost of paternalism had at last found a new corporeal host.

A manic crescendo such as commenced in 1933 in Germany is not answerable to reason. It is tense and terror-ridden. It cannot capitalize on its great capacities, because they seem inadequate. For consciousness of capacity cannot in those circumstances reassure, nor can it satisfy the need to have what others have. Because there are no colonies, industrial effort must be diverted from consumer goods to military materiél for the purpose of gaining possession of raw materials and weaker peoples for exploitation. Because Jews and Poles and Czechs are of different origin, they may have something the Germans do not have, so they are suspect and must be humiliated and destroyed. Because the Christian churches offer security which does not derive from the Nazi paternalism, they are a threat to national security. Because the German people have failed to find long-term satisfaction in peace and are unable to accept themselves as the equals of others or others as their equals, they must turn again and again to the motto of the Great Elector: "Alliances may be all very well, but power of your own is better."

The history of Japan is essentially a picture of internal struggle, of introversion, except for two humiliating periods within the last four hundred years. It is said that in the third century under an empress named Jingó, of all names, an invasion of Korea was undertaken; but in the main, until the end of the sixteenth century Japanese foreign ventures were commercial and apparently not extensive. Japan was invaded and at first defeated by the Mongols in the thirteenth century but suffered little from foreign inroads. In art and literature and civil government it modeled itself after China. The indigenous Shinto religion was in large measure superseded by or combined with the teachings of Confucius and Buddha. Culturally, Japan was less creative of forms and less original as to ideas than most great nations have been. Men who pursued occupations of peace were regarded as far inferior to the men of war, the *Samurai*, who have imprinted their cultural values on the policy and the attitudes of the Japanese.

The Emperor, whose line is said to date back to 660 B.C., is believed to be descended from the sun goddess and is referred to by his people as "Son of Heaven" or "Heavenly King." Throughout the ages, while strong men often ruled in his name, the Mikado has stood to his people as a great paternal figure. Something of an emperor, something of a pope, something of a god, he has been the virtual prisoner of his own prestige and of the powerful feudal lords who used that prestige.

For a thousand years the *daimyo* or feudatories, ruled the islands and fought among themselves. They were supported by armed bands of *Samurai*, professional fighters, trained from generation to generation in warfare. They were a preferred class, second only to their employers. They evolved a code of war and of conduct and attitudes of combativeness and loyalty which form the ethical and political background of Japan today. Toward the latter part of the Middle Ages, the most powerful of the *daimyo*, the *shogun*, not only ruled his own rich domain, but in the name of the emperor conducted the affairs of the national government. He had force and the propaganda power of the Son of Heaven at his command. Nevertheless, there were feudal lords with their bands of *Samurai* whom even the great *shoguns* could never subdue.

In the fifteenth century Portuguese and Spanish missionaries and traders, and to a lesser extent Dutch and British merchants, came to Japan. Having little pride of authorship, the Japanese were tolerant to the new religious ideas and eager for the merchandise of the Indies and the techniques of the Occident. But the struggles between the Jesuits, representing Portugal, and the Franciscans, representing Spain, and the intolerance of the Jesuits and their converts in the destruction of the Buddhist temples and the persecution of Buddhist priests started a movement to exclude all foreigners. When the Shimabara Revolt occurred and the rebels fought under flags bearing the cross and with battle cries of "Jesus," "Maria" and "St. Iago," the *shogun* decided the country had had enough of foreigners. Furthermore, the belief grew that the missionaries were in effect what we would call fifth columnists on behalf of the imperial ambitions of Portugal and Spain.

Following these incidents, for more than two hundred years Japan went into retreat. No foreigner might enter the land, with the exception of one small, ill-treated Dutch trading post, and no Japanese might leave the islands. No seagoing vessel was even permitted to be built. And so the Japanese spirit, which had not trusted itself to depart far from the cultural models of China, now distrusted itself in foreign intercourse.

Before this period of isolation began, there was one more important Japanese contact with the continent of Asia. Under the great *shogun* Hideyoshi in 1592, Japan invaded Korea to find an outlet for the warlike *Samurai* in the interests of internal peace. After a brilliant campaign, in strategy similar to that employed by the Japanese in Malaya, Hideyoshi's troops conquered Korea. Carelessness with regard to lines of communication and indifference to naval power, together with Chinese intervention, resulted in the defeat of the Japanese forces and the eventual recalling of the expedition. Thus, shortly before the period of isolation, when Japan became what H. G. Wells called "these islands of empty romance," it was humiliated by its continental neighbors in the one field in which it had shown initiative and originality. All it had for its sacrifices were the ears and noses of some 38,000 Chinese killed in battle.

When more than two hundred years later, Japan opened its ports again, it did so under the threat of American sea power and after British guns had blasted the fortifications of a *daimyo* who had fired on British ships. Fear and defeat had closed the doors, and gunpowder had opened them.

Now the most bigoted isolationists were no longer in favor of excluding foreigners, but of importing all their methods and inventions which might prove useful to Japan. It was as though, the medieval concept of exclusion being outdated, Japan sought modern ways to avoid domination. Forced into the world, practically blown out of its introversion, Japan commenced a career dedicated to achieving self-sufficiency rather than co-operation or the assumption of mutual responsibility with other nations. In this career it was encouraged by the imperialistic examples of the European nations in China and by the United States in the South Pacific. The Japanese people have been entrenched in their feeling of isolation by the Anglo-American attitude of superiority toward peoples not of the white race and by our fear-ridden exclusion acts and West Coast statutes prohibiting land ownership by Oriental peoples.

In 1867 the *shogunate*, which had already become feeble, was ended, and a few years later the feudal system was abolished upon payment of damages to the *daimyo* by the imperial government; and the *Samurai* as such disappeared. A parliamentary form of government was established. Suffrage was gradually granted to virtually all men of twenty-five. Compulsory education was instituted. Great industrial development and vast commercial enterprises were undertaken and became concentrated in a few great trusts controlled by a few great families. And the spirit of feudalism and the *Samurai* tradition survived.

In their excellent book, *The Far East*, Quigley and Blakeslee write of that period:

> While the Emperor was restored to the seat of power when the shogun vacated it, he was not restored to power. The great *daimio* or the more vigorous *samurai* simply dropped outworn titles and methods of administration to assume the new offices and control the new councils. They saw to it that the Diet should be inferior to the cabinet, the cabinet inferior to the Privy Council, and that all three should be controlled by a half-dozen wise men from their own rank, the *Genro*. They dominated the army and navy and reserved to the military authorities the right to advise the Emperor in matters of national defense. . . . The spread of literacy was nation-wide, but it has had slight political results because of this traditional devotion to the descendants of the *daimio* and the *samurai*. Thus to priority to legal status was added the moral support of popular deference and confidence.

The great political and social changes in Japan in the latter half of the nineteenth century were surface changes. They were at once too shallow to root in any popular movement, and without the power of a popular movement behind them too great to be absorbed at once into the fabric of national attitudes. The men who had been powerful on the feudal estates walked out of their castles and into their banks and offices, where they assumed new power. The *Samurai* were supported no longer by the feudatories out of their personal wealth but in the army and navy out of the national income. No artisan or merchant achieved the respect or influence of the medieval guild merchant. No middle class had the opportunity to develop and take power as it did in western Europe and the United States before the concentration of industrial power. The Emperor, the symbol of the state, was himself semi-divine. There was no coronation oath, such as existed in Europe, which if violated might lead to a dissolution of bonds of loyalty at the instance of the church or the barons. The Mikado never really displaced the power of the feudal lords or absorbed their administrative power in himself as the Tudors did in Britain and the Bourbons in France. There was neither a popular revolution nor a sense in the mass of the people that they had participated in those changes that did take place. The merchants and workers and farmers dealt in and made and bought machine-made goods instead of handmade goods, but they were not instrumental in the industrial revolution which they served.

Nor did the political and economic development of Japan destroy the pattern of family life of its ruling class. The old man—or, in his absence, the old woman—is in very fact the head of the family, whose consent is required for marriage, education or career. He is entitled to formal respect which at times is ritualistic. This requires suppression of self-expression and development, a poor medium for growth of the culture of democracy. The family patriarchate is repeated in the attitude of the people to their Mikado and again in the Privy Council, that powerful semi-feudal body, which until the war, at any rate, could make and break governments.

As is the case with Germany, there can be little hope of retrieving the Japanese people from their career of compulsive aggression short of breaking their ancient family pattern. Democratization must begin with the family. Such reform is possible either through a long-term program of education stimulated from the outside, or through a fundamental revolution of the people which will overthrow the old patterns, which will free a nation of individuals from the burden of national and family paternalism.

The Japanese experience with peoples beyond the threshold had not been reassuring, so the pressure of those working in the *Samurai* pattern found little resistance, and the nation sought security from the external world, which Japan distrusted and which distrusted Japan, in aggressions against the Koreans, the Chinese, the Russians and now all the Allied Nations. Internally, the Japanese found security in their belief in the divine origin of their emperor and the paternalistic system of a neo-feudal fascism. For in Japan "the supreme command is a commission form of dictatorship" and has been; and all the political maneuverings have been only to determine whether the feudalists in uniform or those in the banks and factories were to control.

National self-sufficiency, whether military, economic or intellectual, like individual self-sufficiency, must in the long run prove sterile or self-destructive. Like the individual who seeks to be sufficient to himself for fear of demeaning or sullying himself or because his hatreds cause him to prepare himself for the time when he will release the destructive forces suppressed within him, the drive for national self-sufficiency stems from the fear of intercourse with the ideas and goods of others and the hate-ridden fear of other nations. The results are the Lamas of Lhasa, the Germany of Hitler or the Japan of the *Samurai* tradition.

Like the man who must be dynamic father and comforting mother to his family, must be the bride at every wedding, the corpse at every funeral and cannot bear comparison with his neighbors, the totalitarian leadership cannot endure competition within the national family or without. It is in a flutter between self-sufficiency and jealousy, between escaping from and destroying the outside.

In his work on *Wayward Youth*, August Aichhorn writes:

> When we look at dissocial behaviour, or symptoms of delinquency, as distinct from delinquency, we see the same relation as that between the symptoms of a disease and the disease itself. This parallel enables us to regard truancy, vagrancy, stealing, and the like as symptoms of delinquency, just as fever, inflammation, and pain are symptoms of disease. If the physician limits himself to clearing up symptoms, he does not necessarily cure the disease. The possibility of a new illness may remain; new symptoms may replace the old. In the re-education of the delinquent, we have an analogous situation. Our task is to remove the cause

rather than to eliminate the overt behaviour. Although this seems obvious, it is little understood. Our experience in the guidance clinic and in the training school is that the *symptoms* of delinquency and the fundamental problem underlying delinquency are constantly confused. What parents undertake by way of correction or punishment serves only to suppress the dissocial behaviour.

When we speak of dealing with the German or Japanese nations we too are inclined to think in terms of treating overt behavior rather than causes. We talk in terms of annihilation, disarmament, punishment of Nazi leaders, feeding the hungry, refinancing industry, eliminating the need to fight for raw materials. We want to be at once men of vengeance and men of sentimentality, the father with the rod administering the spanking, the mother fairly oozing with affection for the returned, post-war prodigal. If we look at the long history of the dissocial behavior of Germany among the nations and peoples of the earth, we should be warned against any superficial disposition of the German problem. We must consider psychological causes, not just persons and economics.

When Hitler is overthrown or if he dies, to what can we look forward as the probable reaction of the German people? If he dies without defeat by assassination or from illness, is it not probable that he will be regarded by his people as wearing an halo? Is it not likely that there will grow up a messianic legend, a hope that the great father will return? There is a refrain to an irreverent song about Hitler that goes like this:

Frederick Barbarossa had a great red beard;
Paperhanger Hitler has a teeny weeny moustache.

Yet the teeny weeny moustache may become as great a rallying point for the anxieties of a humiliated people as was the great red beard of Barbarossa. Then the collapse of Nazi Germany might leave a residual memory of triumph which could grow to fantastic proportions and in the future stimulate new moves toward empire and new releases of suppressed barbarism. It was, after all, the lingering glories of the great Napoleon that made possible the reactionary dictatorship of Napoleon III.

If Hitler's fall is brought about by defeat at the hands of the United Nations or through a palace revolution, there are several possibilities. The people may find a new father figure in the person of Comrade Stalin or another Papa Hindenburg culled from the German army and so find protection in a new dictatorship. Or they may revert to the melancholy of the Weimar Republic, or the factional separatism of small states such as existed after the French Revolution. It is possible that they will continue for generations exhausted and emasculated as did Germany following the Thirty Years War. They may on the other hand realize a popular revolution from which a self-confident democracy can grow. The people of Germany may themselves assume responsibility without casting their eyes about for a great man or a great army or a great employer to reassure and protect them.

As we are not treating of an individual delinquent but of millions of individuals with varying hopes and anxieties and experiences and ideals, it is probable that post-war

Germany will present a hodge-podge of all of these possible forms of behavior and more. There will not be identical aims or identical behavior. To the extent that the United Nations consider causes of behavior and psychological tendencies rather than acts and words, they will be able to influence the growth of Germany as a responsible member of the international world.

Undoubtedly a large part of the German population will experience satisfaction with the downfall of Nazi Germany. Release from the *Gestapo* threat and the arbitrariness of the totalitarian state, especially in wartime, will relieve the anxieties of millions of men and women. Adherents to the Catholic and Lutheran churches, the remnants of the Jews, the old Social Democrats, some of the members of the German Communist Party, many of the families of men killed in battle will welcome the destruction of Nazi tyranny. If this large nucleus could by a process of screening be separated from the other parts of the population and given its head, it could establish the foundations of a mature and democratic society in Germany. Though screening is not possible, at the very least the therapeutic program of the United Nations ought to minister to the wounds of this part of the people. It should not include humiliation of them or terror; it should include a chance to find health and means of livelihood and guidance by governments which have had experience in democratic attitudes and practices. Above all, if this section of the German people seeks to realize its freedom from the paternalistic past through revolution, it should not be restrained. For a democratic commonwealth cannot be imposed by armies or carpet-baggers, as the French discovered in Germany and Eastern Europe a hundred and fifty years ago and as the Northern extremists found out after the Civil War. Neither can a free co-operative spirit be achieved by a people suffering from a suppressed longing for paternalism. If our post-war organization cannot make possible a popular assumption of responsibility even by revolutionary means, if we cannot resist playing patriarch to a young democracy, we shall once more throw Germany into melancholy, into one of those emasculated depressions from which it will strive to recover by renewed violence. It will repeat the substitution of violence and barbarism for the satisfactions to be derived from creative effort and the congenial society of other men and nations.

Undoubtedly, too, there will be millions of Germans who will be unreconciled to the deflation of the *Führer Prinzip*. Some of these will be irredentist; they will think that if it had not been for this or that malevolent act of Britain or the Communists or the Pope or the Jews, they would now be in clover: the Aryans would be riding herd. They will be waiting again for *Der Tag*. Others will feel deprived and lost; in their fantasies they will look for a new Leader who by his own forcefulness will impart to them a renewed sense of power and vigor.

How shall these groups be treated? They will be potentially the most dangerous to world peace. They will want to repeat the cruelty they themselves have suffered; they will want the fellowship of the gang and the leadership of the master gangster. They will be the wayward leaven of a wayward nation. If again we could screen these groups out of the remainder of the population, we should re-educate them, in so far as they are re-educable, from their delinquent, dissocial tendencies. Neither a spirit of vengeance nor an attitude of washing our hands of all responsibility for them should prompt the conduct of the United Nations. Anger or revenge on our part will stiffen their resistance, will throw them into the arms of their fantasies for security against new threats and the anxieties resulting from such fantasies. We do not make a social being out of a delinquent boy or girl by anger or vengeance. Here possibly through a reorientation of schooling and guidance by experts from the United Nations, both the irredentist and the lost people of Germany could be helped. If they are to be salvaged they must be accorded a sympathetic understanding of their emotional problems and nevertheless be convinced that they will not be permitted to terrorize their fellows or the world.

How can this be done? It depends largely on whether Germany is occupied by a British and American expeditionary force or by a triumphant Red Army or not occupied at all. It depends, too, on whether a popular revolution occurs in Germany. If there should be no such revolution, the task will be difficult, for we should be confronted with a beaten people who have not developed in themselves and of themselves some positive attitude, an affirmative pattern upon which to build. If such a revolution takes place, it is more probable that with outside encouragement a social Germany will establish itself.

If there is neither a revolution nor an occupation, the situation will be hopeless. For in that case the German people will again evade a realization of their responsibility; they will not be pointed in a new direction nor will they have freed themselves from fantasies of paternalism which would block any appreciation of democratic cooperation. In spite of defeat something would tell them that they had evaded paying a penalty, that they had got away with something.

But armies of occupation have their dangers too. A Soviet army would undoubtedly be accompanied by a sovietization of the country. Stalin might then replace Hitler. While from a democratic point of view this would be undesirable and from a psychological viewpoint it would defer development of maturity in Germany as a nation, it is possible that after the war a greater degree of democracy will be forced on the Communist bureaucracy by the demands of the millions of soldiers and tens of millions of civilians who have suffered and bled in the war. Consequently, while not the most desirable event from the angle of the evolution of a democratic Germany, occupation by the Red Army may not prove as fatal as it at first may seem to be.

The risks of Anglo-American occupation are also not inconsiderable. There is always the possibility that reactionary army men and the pressure of the big industries at home may convert the business of policing into a restoration of the old German trust-monopoly and *Junker* control; or the commercial and financial exploitation of Germany; or the use of Germany as a base for a new war against Soviet Russia; or the imposition of our forms of democratic ideas and procedure on the German people instead of permitting them to work out their own.

A more constructive program would come as the result of prearrangement between the United Nations rather than either a race for Berlin or stopping short of occupying every part of Germany.

Both as retributive justice brought home to the German people and to satisfy the normal desire of the occupied countries to punish the guilty and to remove the symbols of the Nazi regime, the leading Nazis, including the local leaders and *Gauleiter*, should be tried and either executed or imprisoned in exile. An international police force, in which later Germans shall participate, must be maintained, not to sustain a *status quo* or restore a *status quo ante*, but solely to prevent Germany from rearming or fortifying any part of the country. If such an occupying force could be regarded more as a probationary officer is in civil life than as a punitive expedition, the German people would be less humiliated and would more easily be brought to a wholesome attitude toward themselves and other nations.

For this reason, part of the occupying force should be civilian. Its emphasis in the initial stages should be on nutrition and health, but its principal task ought to be the reorganization of German schools and the expert treatment of that part of the population which will suffer psychologically from the destruction of the father-figure. I do not mean that British or Americans or Russians or anyone else should replace Germans in these fields. They cannot succeed if they try to do so. But the civilian corps of occupation can train and guide many Germans who will be leaders in the reorientation of German education.

Even before Hitler and his associates filled the schools with the spew of hatred and the fear of the *Gestapo*, German education in the home and the school drummed into the people a dread-laden overrespect for what was forbidden and for the place of the father in the family, and for teachers and officialdom, who became symbolic of his authority. The very basis of establishing better social characteristics in the German people and freeing them of their subservience to paternalism must be the creation of a new attitude towards authority. Education must be directed towards the creation of greater fellowship in family and school relationships, between parents or teachers and children, and a sense that government is to serve, not to be served. Otherwise they will not develop that attitude towards equality which makes democracy possible and gives a sense of freedom rather than of repression. For when authority is something in which they do not participate, but which they regard as outside of themselves and to be feared, there is little likelihood that those subject to such authority will be able to co-operate with others, for they will be inclined to respect only force.

Undoubtedly the Nazi Youth Movement has to some extent broken the hold of paternal authority. The Party has superseded the father as the final arbiter. This is an important break with German tradition and must be exploited by German postwar education. There is danger, of course, that the reaction from Hitlerism will once more enhance the traditional position of the *pater familias*. To this possibility those in the educational section of the occupying force must be alert. Here they will be on the familiar ground of adolescent psychology.

In the schools and services for children, and in those for adults, it will be important to afford the people opportunities to relieve themselves of their fears and hatreds and release their affectionate and creative instincts. Through the arts and the sciences, in personal and unregimented fields, disappointment can be turned to satisfaction, and the fear of defeat in world competition replaced by achievements in a less aggressive spirit.

Man and child, the great mass of the German people have experienced harshness and brutal discipline. Some penalties they must pay, for it is important that they be brought to understand that their assaults and aggressions cannot be indulged in without retribution. This can best be brought about unemotionally and humanely. But, and I quote once more from Aichhorn:

> If the educator employs even harsher discipline, he is using the same methods which brought the child [or adult] into the original conflict. Thus he strengthens the antagonistic impulses which already existed and increases rather than mitigates the tendency to delinquency.

Good parents and good teachers and here and there a judge know the difference between firmness and harshness. Those who prepare the terms of peace must also understand this difference, for the result of firmness is respect and that of harshness is a desire to kill.

It is not abnormal for people, especially those who do not develop emotionally beyond the adolescent stage, to feel the need for punishment out of a justifiable or imaginary sense of guilt. Unquestionably many Germans will experience this need for punishment. Even when they have not themselves administered the tortures of Dachau and Poland or executed hostages in France, Czechoslovakia and the Balkans, many will have identified themselves with Hitler and his agents. They will feel the need of punishment to expiate their sense of guilt. There will also be a normal demand for vengeance on the part of the conquered peoples, a blood-lust to compensate for torture and ruin, for the death of loved ones and the destruction of loved objects. It is possible that these needs will balance one another through the bombing of German cities and the killing of thousands of Germans in occupied regions once the Nazi power begins to crumble.

It is to be hoped that both this need of punishment and this lust for vengeance will be stilled by the inevitable blood-letting that will accompany German defeat. Otherwise there is danger that, by their subsequent provocative acts, the German people will be inviting punishment and testing their immunity to punishment. The occupied countries also will make reconciliation impossible if they restrain themselves from administering retribution and repeat the die-hard attitude of Clemenceau and Poincaré at the end of the first World War. It is better to punish and be done with it than harass with abuse and odious terms which must keep the vanquished in subjection. The slaughter of many Germans—and of Japanese too—after the war will be unfortunate but not entirely evil, unless it is exploited by politicians into a pogrom or a fixation of hatred which the resumption of normal occupations does not dispel. In such circumstances the letting of the blood of defeated foes will be vicious and dangerous to the victorious and the defeated.

I have already referred to the necessity for adequate diet and health services after the war. Malnutrition and disease lead to sullenness and rebelliousness. They would not establish conditions basic to the creation of healthy attitudes. This is true not only of the wayward nations, but throughout the world. A few nations cannot have a secure living standard if others are inadequately fed and ridden by disease without stimulating a disequilibrium among the nations, a disequilibrium which in turn will stimulate aggression.

It goes without saying that freedom of worship is necessary if the spirits of men and women are not to be further frustrated. This means neither compulsory worship nor interference with worship nor an established church. God can neither be reached under compulsion nor destroyed by it; but compulsion in matters of faith can and does breed resentment. Worship is a form of self-expression and of self-realization and as such must be afforded freedom and protection in any democratic society.

In the first years after the war, there will probably be much recrimination by Germans against Germans and also against their former leaders and foes. No attempt ought to be made to suppress these expressions. They will be part of the stabilizing process, part of recovery of self-respect and a necessary discharge of pent-up hatred. Nor should we hasten to remove all possible grounds for complaint. Because a child is not to be thrashed is no reason for spoiling him or permitting him to escape the reasonable consequences of his acts so long as those consequences derive from his act and not from someone else's passion or desire to exhibit power. Many grounds for complaint will doubtless arise, not from the apparent devastations and penalties of the war, but from the power conflicts within and without the country, though the war, its causes and results will be used as grounds for complaint. But among free men there is no substitute for patient analysis of the factual and emotional factors involved in such complaint. How many times have we not witnessed attempts to suppress protest result in grotesque magnification of the alleged evils attacked?

The semidivine regard in which the emperor is held and the stronger umbilical cord that ties the Japanese social organization to feudalism, make the problem of democratizing Japan seem more difficult than that of Germany. And any attempt by occidentals to step in to reorganize Japan would be fatal. We should consider that, from a psychological point of view, the Japanese urge to free itself from the paternalism of the white races is healthy. Should Great Britain or the United States or the Russians step in to control Japan proper, after the war, they might crush the most promising point of departure for the attainment of Japanese maturity.

It would seem wiser, therefore, to place the Chinese partner in the Allied cause—or the Indies—in charge of the dismantling of Japanese war industry and the necessary policing. The ancestral relationship of Chinese culture to the Japanese would also indicate the advisability of introducing Chinese as counselors in the revamping of the Japanese educational system. While Chinese may intervene with better grace and hope of avoiding some of the fundamental animosities which white intervention would involve, this is no sure cure, no key to the hearts of the Japanese. For many Japanese undoubtedly have a special animosity toward the Chinese because they are indebted to the Chinese for so much of their culture.

No basic reform of Japan appears to be a realistic probability without a popular, indigenous revolution which will do to the vestiges of feudal and imperial power and to the *Samurai* culture what the revolution under Cromwell and the Revolution of 1688 did in Britain, and what the American, the French and the Russian revolutions did in those countries. The break with paternalism must be so definite and so widespread that it will become a part of the thinking of all levels of the nation and of every one of its local institutions.

So for some time, perhaps long, perhaps short, wayward Japan must be prevented from repeating aggressive action until it is prepared to reform itself. As in the case of Germany, this prevention ought to be accomplished with a conscious effort to avoid humiliation. It should be carried out firmly but in a spirit less of vengeance than of instruction, to the effect that the world will not tolerate international disorderly conduct.

It is not improbable that a victorious Red Army in the Far East will result in a victory of the Communists in China and a communist revolution in Japan. Again as with Germany, this would not be the most desirable result for it would substitute a Stalin for the Mikado and a party bureaucracy for the *daimyo* and their *Samurai;* but in terms of development this substitution would represent progress as a break with a tradition of aggression and an end of that spiritual conservatism which is only capable of translating ancient power into new political mechanisms.

It is believed by some, not without reason, that if the armed forces of Japan are defeated, Hirohito may take power into his hands directly. With the prestige of his divine descent he may then become a dictator in the western style. But it is questionable whether that prestige would not be risked and rebellion on the part of the people and the army invited if the United Nations blockaded a defeated Japan. If the Emperor were to descend to mundane dictatorship it would go far towards liquidating his claim to divinity. We have witnessed in Russia with what rapidity a well-disciplined revolutionary party can disregard the religious appendages of government when the government itself is inadequate.

The extent to which the Axis countries should be permitted to join other peoples in the conduct of international affairs and the degree to which assistance should be rendered to permit a revival of peaceful industry, are subjects better treated under a discussion of postwar world organization than here. However, these points should be suggested: that, as the Axis nations achieve responsible self-government, their healthy growth could be encouraged by gradually giving them a share of responsibility in the councils of the world; that the mistakes of punitive reparations should not again be repeated; and that for an indefinite period the Axis nations should not be trusted with those industries which are capable of producing arms. The airplane industry, plants for the production of heavy metals and the chemical industry should be dismantled in those countries. The balance of productivity could be shifted by reducing the production of other goods in Allied lands in the interest of encouraging industries in the Axis nations which would permit economic recovery without making rearmament possible.

Security and peace require sacrifice and generosity and

self-restraint by those in power even more than by the vanquished. Nations, like individuals, must be able to forego immediate rewards and spoils for long-term satisfactions. This will be the kernel of genuine reconstruction.

7

International Democracy and Biting off More Than One Can Chew

THE PRECEDING CHAPTERS have demonstrated that we dare not take institutions or words at their face values because they are in reality tools of the human search for satisfactions and symbols of human valuations. Such ideas as liberty, equality, fraternity, democracy; such institutions as majority rule, capitalism, communism, gain meaning in terms of ethical and psychological ends. Men who have the capacity to find their major satisfactions in creativeness and collaboration will make something creative and co-operative out of the tools they use. On the other hand, men who must be aggressive and competitive and destructive will find another sense and a different objective for phrase and institution, which will become not tools as much as weapons for them. And men who have the need to feel driven or patronized will find the security of rewards and punishments in the same words and institutions.

Mankind has been largely composed of people who needed power—not as security against aggression, but as a way of quelling anxieties in themselves as to their own inadequacy—and of people who must find assurance in a channel buoyed by rewards on the right hand and punishments on the left. Thus, the institutional tone of the world has been for the most part pitched to ears trained to hear the tread of power. Therefore we speak and think of world organization mostly in terms of power and degrees of law enforcement. We slur over matters of psychology, as though the mental and emotional lives of men and women and children were of little account, as though they were divisible from the physical aspects of life, such as force and bread and gold.

Consequently, when we speak of a league of nations as a sort of superstate or federation, our eyes tend to be bigger than our stomachs. To the extent that we shall try to realize a dream of international law enforced by an international police, while we ignore our human relationships and our mutually interdependent attitudes, we shall be biting off more than we can chew. We say that Wilson's League of Nations failed because it lacked the power of law enforcement, and that the next league must have more power. We talk of Germany and Japan building on power and of France letting it slip from her hands. But what power? And why power? While we ignore the why of the power-quest and the why of the confusion between equality and identity, we shall continue to assume that all men mean the same things by the same words and want the same results from similar institutions. We avoid finding and facing these psychological causes, although we know that it is only through gaining knowledge of the nature of physical force and power that we have been able to make it serviceable to man.

This assumption that there is no multiple meaning in words, that men must keep their engagements, except they speak in bad faith, and the collateral assumption that institutions have but a single purpose, have led to repeated disillusionment and distrust. We may come upon unpleasant surprises when we say to cannibals, "How about something to eat?" Because we differed in our ends and in our understanding of each other's ends, and because the causes of our respective purposes were never mutually understood, we have tended to jump to the conclusion that we or others have failed or that we or they have been deceitful.

Nevertheless, we go right on and pattern our blueprints on the smug and cynical hypothesis that human nature is always the same—meaning that on the whole human nature is not good and that as it is static someone must always be in the position to bludgeon or father someone else who would otherwise be nothing except destructive. From this we assume that if we can establish an equilibrium in the use of force and in economic dominion, we shall have done all that can be done. We may differ as to what this equilibrium shall be and who shall maintain it, but we do not question that someone must do so until the Messiah comes or the day of judgment arrives or the mystical masses reform of their own accord when the last bourgeois has been eliminated.

But is such a fatalistic view of human nature the only possible hypothesis on which we can build? Certainly it conflicts with the democratic hypothesis. It denies the validity of any belief in ethical ends and the modification of human behavior into ethical patterns. It is contradicted by the findings of psychiatry, that the attitudes of people can be diverted from destructive channels to those in which greater satisfactions are found in co-operative relationships and the development of individual capacities free of anxieties as to their inadequacy. This does not mean that men will be unworried though the wolf be at the door or untroubled though the loaded gun be at their backs or unperturbed when some loved one is suffering from cancer. But it does imply that men can meet the threats of hunger or physical danger or fatal disease for what they are, not as punishments for guilt or weakness, not as forces compelling them to seek power and to destroy others in order to reassure themselves, so as to escape from anxiety, and not as reasons to surrender themselves to the dominion of others.

We have all read of the story of the three fliers who lived for thirty-four days in a rubber boat, without supplies of water or food, on a storm-shocked and shark-ridden sea, and who, though weak and suffering, walked upright on the shore of the island on which they beached because they would not crawl in the possible presence of enemies. This, too, is human nature. We know what men and women through the ages have been ready to endure for children and for faith. The mother who will protect her children at any sacrifice of herself, the men who found the cure for yellow fever, the Pilgrims, the men, women and children in Nazi-occupied Europe who have defied the totalitarian sadism of the Nazis—they, too, are testimonials of human nature.

Human nature, then, need be neither craven nor destructive. And the institutions of men can be developed with an eye to encouraging rather than discouraging independence, co-operation and creativity. That in essence is what we mean when we say that we want to develop a democratic world: we want to develop institutions founded on attitudes congenial to the survival and enrichment of human integrity.

Consequently, it is not enough to develop blueprints for world peace and international organization which treat of power and wealth and ignore attitudes and individuals. In the development of secure and stable international society, we must stimulate and encourage those attitudes and instrumentalities which tend towards self-reliant and co-operative individuals and groups and which discourage those attitudes and institutions which tend towards paternalism and the drive to achieve or to impose either identical conditions or aggressive competition.

For example: If in accordance with the commitment of the Atlantic Charter raw materials were to be pooled, this could be a democratic step to assure nonproducers of items such as tin, nickel, cotton, coffee and wool some proportionate access to those commodities. Such a pooling could, however, be imperialistic insofar as the development of the sources of raw materials are concerned. They could be produced by quasi-slave labor under conditions in which the natives would have no opportunity to participate in the benefits of the production or the determination of wages or the standard of living under which they would work and rest and rear families. There is little in the record of the imperialism of Great Britain, the United States, the

Netherlands or the Axis powers to indicate solicitude for the dignity, or recognition of the equality, of peoples in exploited regions. Nevertheless, the stability of the world and the development of a democratic society are contingent upon the attitude with which the nations handle the pooling of raw materials.

Another example: The great nations of Europe and the Americas can treat yellow and brown and black peoples with the formal respect of the diplomatic idiom, or they can accept them as equals in fact. The grant of equal rights, as we have seen in the minority treaties signed by the central European countries at Versailles, is a fiction where realization of such rights is garroted on an emotional barrier against the acceptance of variation. Here again, although the dominant groups of the white races have treated the colored peoples on an equality with less fortunate white men and women insofar as profit making and concubinage are concerned, the record reeks with patronage and discrimination. Nor does it promise well that the majority parties in Britain and the United States today may control the first steps in peace-making. For most of the British tories and most of the southern Democrats represent an anachronism in democratic society, a vermiform appendix, inflamed with a chronic irritation at the thought of equality between peoples of different color. Like the appendix in the human body which destroys the body's effectiveness and welfare when it cuts up, those bigotry-infected members threaten to impede the effectiveness and welfare of democratic society. For the failure to take an equalitarian attitude towards those races which are not white, and which have been subject races, will be the measure of the failure to appraise the current world-wide revolution and to recognize that the colored peoples are struggling to attain their maturity by freeing themselves of the paternalism of the white peoples.

One further example of the importance of attitudes in the development of secure and stable international society, and also a test of the *bona fides* of our devotion to the principles of democracy: With the end of the war there will unquestionably be a breakdown of the authority which controls the Axis nations, their allies and their occupied territories. What will be the attitude of the conquerors toward such revolutionary crises? Will they play the part the Allies played in the abortive Spartacist Revolution in Germany in 1918? Will there be duplications of the Archangel fiasco and the subsidizing of the counter-revolutionary movement in Russia? Will the Soviet Government attempt to convert rebellion into communist revolution? Will the victors invite a new group of reactionaries—perhaps with the connivance of Quisling Nazis, Fascists or Japanese—into the seats of power, as they did when the Bourbons were restored to the throne of France after Napoleon was defeated? Then the revolution was suppressed by the Allies of 1814 and 1815 with the connivance of Talleyrand; and Lafayette, writing to Jefferson of this piece of paternalism, said with regret: "I wanted a National insurrection against domestic despotism the Succès of which would lead to a treaty with or a Spirited attack Upon the foreigners—in Both cases we were the Masters of our own Government."

We must come to realize that in most lands it is only

through popular revolutions that people will become able to take affairs out of the hands of those who have dominated them and become the masters of their own governments. It will be only as they achieve the independence to make treaties with foreign nations or are prepared to drive them out that they will be free of encroachments from abroad.

Thus after freeing herself from the Japanese *Samurai*, China also must assure herself of freedom from the old set-up of treaty ports and tariff concessions to foreign powers. The American and British declarations on this point must be broadened and reformed. Then sooner or later China will need to complete the revolution commenced under Sun Yat-sen. For in spite of his revolutionary program, and that of the ruling Kuomintang party, China has few of the freedoms associated with free peoples or democratic states, not freedom of speech nor press nor assemblage; nor for that matter a wide or controlling suffrage.

The old way of imperialism was to punish nations which sought to free themselves. So after the Opium War and the Boxer Rebellion in China and the Sepoy Mutiny in India, penalties in the form of indemnities or customs controls were instituted. Smaller attempts at freedom were met with local acts of brutality, behavior which would have broken any government of a democratic state if attempted in small measure at home.

One of the interesting phenomena in the growth of democratic states is that at the same time they maintained respectable, if not always equitable, marriages with industry at home, their imperialist commerce on the next continent was generally a shabby, sadistic and illicit affair. It was only distance that made the democratic and imperialist menages compatible. But the showdown has come. Owen Lattimore, advisor to Chiang Kai-shek, writes:

> The survival of democracy demands the spread of democracy, and the spread of democracy means the end of imperialism, the end of the integrated imperialism-and-democracy to which we have so long been accustomed.

It would be inaccurate to suggest that imperialism made a lie of democratic claims. Nor was it just a subterfuge to insist upon the test of "fitness for self-government" as a condition to granting independence to subject peoples. Undoubtedly there are, as there were for centuries, powerful groups in imperialistic countries whose interests lead them to give only lip service to democracy and who know the will-o'-the-wisp character of the test of fitness for self-government as a key to freedom. But by and large people have not been conscious of any difference between their expressed democracy and their achieved imperialism. For centuries the white man had no question as to his superiority, although he admitted that that superiority involved a correlative duty known as the White Man's Burden. Although there may have been some confusion between the duty on the one hand of bringing the white man's civilization and morals to less highly developed peoples and selling goods and spreading white men's social diseases on the other, perfectly decent people have assumed that the evils incident to the "civilizing" process were due to the lack of understanding and of moral restraint on the part of backward peoples. Being possessed of greater military strength, greater self-confidence and more finished goods, white men attained dominion over others. And dominion necessarily means the assumption of moral superiority.

It would be a mistake to assume that all nineteenth- and twentieth-century imperialism has been brutal or abusive. It was so when that was deemed necessary in order to retain prestige and authority. Customarily, however, imperialism was condescending towards the darker-hued brethren. It tried contemporaneously to save their souls by a civilized method—possibly confusing to barbarians—of speaking of peace and salvation in biblical phrases while brandishing a gun, and pending salvation by driving hard bargains for labor and for wealth. But in spite of the predominantly pacific moments in colonial life, and in spite of many improvements in the way of public health and transportation and considerable, though not necessarily general, improvement in colonial standards of living, imperialism has undoubtedly seemed brutal and abusive to the natives—possibly more brutal and abusive than in fact it was just because it was contradictory, repressive and patronizing. It discouraged self-development on the part of the dominated peoples. We know in a more familiar field that parents need not be cruel to their children to create in them the fixed notion that they are injured by their parents. When children are forbidden to express their own opinions and ambitions, and when they are denied the fruits of their own labors, there is at least a scintilla of justice to the belief that they are being abused. For it is abuse to restrain self-development of individuals or groups, abuse no less real because it is psychological and its results therefore more subtle than are those inflicted by starvation and the lash.

During two hundred years of occupation of India the British have made no serious effort to make the Indian people "fit for self-government." Nor have the Dutch in hundreds of years made such an attempt in Java, or the Belgians in the Congo or the French in Indo-China or the Germans in the Cameroons. Latin Americans, fit or not fit, achieved self-government—mostly local dictatorships, it is true—by their own efforts in spite of Spain and Portugal. And by our adherence to the Monroe Doctrine we have proclaimed that it is closer to democracy to have your own home-grown autocrat than have the status of crown colonies.

Thus the colonial system, whether exercised through sovereignty, spheres of influence or extra-territoriality, is a denial of equality, and as such is a threat to peace and a contradiction of democracy. Any *bona fide* democratic peace, any attempt to remove fundamental causes of unrest must contemplate the acknowledgment of the political equality of all peoples and include an educational program aimed at the acceptance of equality between men and women who are different in color, religion, cultural background and custom.

If with the reconquest of conquered islands and territories, the United Nations assume the immediate task of maintaining order and reviving industry, they cannot hope to create a harmonious world without promptly adopting a timetable of emancipation. This is the most concrete way of saying: "We shall consider you our equals. We hope you will succeed; but if you don't, if you make mistakes—

don't we all?" The pattern of the liberation of the Philippines is a good model. The old subjective test of the fitness of a colonial people for self-government is deceptive and must be discarded. Being subjective, it necessarily arouses paternalistic defensive patterns in any nation which has dominion over colonial people.

We know that, in addition to selfish economic interests, the paternalistic pattern is apt to contain the anxiety that loss of dominion means loss of strength and vigor and security. These selfish interests and these anxieties are bound to contribute to the definition of fitness for self-government unless a timetable for liberation is definitely set. It is the failure to set such a timetable and the distrust of darker races thus implied, which has been largely responsible for the distrust by the people of India of the promises of Great Britain to grant freedom to India after the threat of Japanese invasion has passed. It is this failure, too, more even than the economic drain of war, that threatens the substance of the British Empire and the hope of a British Commonwealth of Nations which will include the members of the Empire who are not predominantly of Anglo-Saxon origin.

Any attempt to recreate a white hegemony will inevitably alarm China, for it will indicate to her that extra-territoriality may crawl out of the ruins of the International Settlement in Shanghai and the wreck of the feeble fortresses of Hong Kong. The revivial of imperialism in Malaya and the Dutch East Indies, the failure to adopt a program of freedom for the Pacific and Indian Ocean regions will make certain what is now only a strong possibility—that China will throw in her lot with the Soviet Union or even with Japan after the withdrawal of Japanese troops from Chinese soil.

One of the genuine achievements of Stalinist Russia is the implementing of the principle of nationality which Stalin developed under Lenin's guidance. Tartars, Georgians, Mongols and Jews are on an equality with Muscovite Russians in the recognition of their respective cultures and languages, in economic well-being and educational opportunity and advancement in the state. Discrimination is a punishable and punished offense. This is a doctrine which must appeal to the darker peoples of Asia, Africa and Latin America, and which in time will isolate the white nations of Europe and North America.

The Soviet principle of nationality must not be confused with that of nationalism. Nationalism is not a principle of mutual respect but of introversion. It developed as a unifying force and accelerated the breakdown of feudalism. It became a neo-clannishness throughout the mercantile, industrial and finance-capitalist eras, until at last it developed into a veritable goiter to the hyperthyroid Axis powers. It is worth noting that Germany and Italy were the last of the great powers to attain nationhood and that Japan was the last power to emerge from traditional feudalism. They entered the world of power humiliated and suffering from an inner compulsion to prove their own power. They have used their nationalism as a form of self-flagellation to whip themselves into achieving equality with other nations—equality in the field of aggression and exploitation.

One thing is plain, that the psychology of the aggressor compels him to be always on the defensive. Someone has an advantage over him; someone scorns him; someone is out to get him. So he must show the other fellow his prowess; he must humiliate those who scorn him; he must try to get what others have whether it be appropriate to his capacities or resources or not. Abdul Abulbul Emir and Ivan Skavinsky Skavar must resent every incident as a personal affront and exhibit their own strength and daring though it be the death of them.

It is this fundamentally defensive attitude of the aggressor—this incipient where not actual paranoia—which, as Lenore G. Marshall has pointed out, is the reason why the aggressor nation can claim to be fighting defensive wars and believe it. The aggressor claims to be encircled and believes it. Encirclement is in most instances a subjective matter. A man with claustrophobia feels encircled in a subway train or an elevator. The normal man does not. Japan surrounded by water felt encircled; England did not. Germany in the midst of armed nations felt encircled; Switzerland did not. Italy, with a barrier of mountains on the north and the Mediterranian on all her other borders, felt encircled; Greece did not. Psychiatrists suggest that there is a connection between claustrophobia and a sense of guilt. Is there not a probable relationship between the claim of encirclement and that guilt feeling which comes from aggression? It is a not uncommon psychological trick to bring about the very situation one fears as a justification for having such fear. The hypochondriac fears disease; he makes himself sick and then he can say with truth, "You see—I told you so." It is common, too, for one with guilt feelings to create a situation which will justify himself in his own eyes. Subtly he will irritate others to the first overt word or act of aggression. The prospective enemy mobilizes his defense; that becomes a cause of war, a satisfaction of guilt feelings to the already mobilized aggressor. Germany, Italy and Japan have indeed become encircled. They were driven to bring about such encirclement in self-justification.

The vicious circle of feelings of inadequacy leading to aggression following through to guilt and a renewed sense of inadequacy rationalized into reasons to be aggressive, can only be broken if somewhere along the line reality is brought into focus. Essential to any long-term program of peace, then, is an educational campaign which will bring peoples to a sense of their adequacy, to a realization and development of their capacities, and to a conviction that there is therefore no need to be defensive and aggressive. This, of course, means that those with power, the victors in war, must give a factual basis to such an educational program by abstaining from threatening or exploiting those with little or no military or economic protection. This is not too much to expect of nations any more than it is of individuals. It is not fear of the police which restrains most people from stealing candy from children or shoving the blind under a motorbus.

Aggressive nationalism has led to the program of the self-contained state. Sooner or later someone calls the bluff of a bully. When some threatened nation refuses to bow to intimidation, the bully must be prepared to fight or to lose prestige. Unless a *Blitzkrieg*, fought on prepared reserves, is successful, the aggressor to fight at all must be in a position to withstand attrition. This involves blockade or counter-blockade and the protection of lines of communications to food and the raw materials necessary for the furnaces of industry. Therefore, if an aggressor nation is not to back water at the first substantial opposition, it must be as nearly self-contained as possible. Germany in 1914 and in 1939, cut off from the greater world of raw materials, could not have undertaken wars, knowing the possibility that they might last for years, had it not believed that it had sufficient stock piles to sustain itself to victory. Contrariwise, it was not prepared at Algeciras in 1906 and lost face when the Kaiser had to back down. Russia, with its aggressive political policy in a world that feared and hated communism, also had to attempt self-sufficiency. Japan had been building up reserves for years—probably ever since it was required to disgorge Shantung at the close of the first World War—before it attacked the United States and Great Britain. Mussolini, of course, thought the war was in the mopping-up stage when Italy attacked France, and so was unprepared.

The attempt to achieve self-sufficiency arises from the identical sense of inadequacy which gives rise to aggression. It is an attempt to find adequacy in the power of possession rather than in material endowments and the development and the interplay of such endowments with those of other people. Whether such endowments be personal capacities or the wealth of nations, the patterns are much the same: either they must be enjoyed for what they are through the processes of development and exchange; or they must be used for the purpose of quelling anxieties by means of the cultivation of prestige and the practice of competitive force; or they must be left in their virgin state, unrisked and unrealized. The drive to achieve self-sufficiency is an attempt to attain an artificial situation and actually impedes the development of capacities and the realization of satisfactions in daily living. It requires no proof for anyone to see that if the economic systems of the Axis powers and of the Soviet Union had not been devoted for so many years to the attainment of self-sufficiency, to building up stock piles of materials useful for war only, this wealth and those efforts could have been used for public improvements and consumer goods which would have benefited the people at home and abroad.

It is not through self-sufficiency, but through development and exchange, that nations have progressed. Feudalism broke down largely because the manor could no longer remain self-sufficient economically or emotionally. The tempting goods of the itinerant merchant and the lure of slaughtering infidels were much too enticing for manorial isolation to be maintained. In the mercantile period the ideal of self-sufficiency was expanded to include colonial possessions. The struggle between Great Britain and the American colonies revolved largely around the concept of a self-sufficient British Empire. The American Revolution and the precedent smuggling trade with the French and Spanish colonies cracked mercantile self-sufficiency, until finally Great Britain found that the gates to success were her own gates and that by throwing them wide open through free trade she could achieve more economic wealth than any people had possessed and more security at home and abroad than had any nation since Rome.

Other nations which reached the stage of industrialism later, felt themselves too insecure to follow Britain's example. They were not content to buy cotton goods from

Manchester and steel from Sheffield. They were not willing to risk the prices of monopoly. They sought to make themselves self-sufficient through the medium of tariff walls. But these walls were also cracked, and in the country which had achieved the greatest development under the protection of tariffs, the United States. For the Smoot-Hawley Tariff Act of 1930, which increased already high tariffs, made it impracticable for debtors of the United States to pay their obligations and made it impossible to attain rapidly a new stable balance of prices of raw materials after the inflation bubble broke in 1929. The high-tariff trend of the United States has been stopped and tentatively reversed through the Hull trade agreements. These have made it possible to lower specific schedules to a point which would permit other countries to sell products in the United States in exchange for tariff reductions which permit American products to enter those countries. From a long-term point of view, such a tariff policy offers at least two possibilities: first, that greater stability can be developed in what has historically been a highly unstable American economic order; and secondly, the development of a national rather than a lobbyist attitude toward import duties.

Tariffs are barriers and, like all barriers, they evidence distrust. There is no question that, as the affairs of nations have been conducted, there has been good reason for lack of trust. The economic need is the same in this respect as the political—that is, the development of such institutions and such attitudes as will give confidence. The world of commerce depends upon credit, and credit depends upon faith. The credit structure of the capitalist economy has been severely mauled. The most secure countries have devaluated their currency, almost all have defaulted on some or all of their obligations. The overload which war indebtedness is placing upon the earning power of the future makes it almost inevitable that further defaults will follow, and the sooner war debts are written off as a cost of war along with lost loves and destroyed materials, the sooner will the world be able to settle down to economic stability. For the uncertainty whether debts will be paid and the burden of taxes to meet even the interest rates on government debts and the lure of inflation will be a drain on future earnings and a strain on the consciences of peoples. They will want to wipe out the past so that they may be freer to address themselves to the present, but at the same time will feel inhibited from attaining such freedom by the desire to keep their promises. Yet a frank acknowledgment of governmental insolvency the world over is the only hope of achieving postwar stability. Economic stability must be a foundation pile of any system of security, of any economic system or systems which are not to upset international balance and recharge the circuit of fear and aggression.

It is too much, however, to expect tariffs to be abandoned at the drop of the weapons of war, just as it is too much to expect universal disarmament. Men will prolong their supposed advantages as far as possible, and by means of those weapons with which they are familiar. The problem before us is not primarily disarmament and the establishment of free trade, but the adoption of a program which will enable different peoples to have confidence in themselves and each other and to divert their aggressions into constructive development and interchange.

Another form of barrier which has interrupted peaceable interchange is restriction on migration. Prohibitions on immigration and emigration, and quota provisions, limit the intercourse of peoples. This barrier also is caused by distrust and by the desire not to have to share with others where shortages exist. It is a barrier created by the fear that new immigrants will lower the living standard and that emigrants will impoverish the land they leave. No ready solution can be offered for this problem. Men are not to be cured by fiat of those anxieties which arise because other people are different. Nor is the acceptance of other people on a basis of equality to be achieved by swamping labor markets. But once more, a conscious effort must be made to eradicate the fear of difference and to absorb into productive effort those millions of men and women who live on the margin of starvation even though they talk a different language and are of another color. An intelligent approach is the arrangement between Mexico and the United States for the temporary admission into the latter country of Mexican farm laborers. This presents dangers, of course, because if these itinerant workers are exploited financially or compelled to live in a substandard way, new barriers of fear and hate will be created. However, it is possible that international organization can be such as to reduce these dangers to a minimum. The imported worker could be made secure against exploitation; the native worker against a lowered standard. If, for example, some such body as the International Labor Office were to be granted by the treaties of peace powers of initiation to facilitate the emigration of workers, the means of investigation and publicity, and the right to enforce minimum standards in national courts, surplus labor supply might safely be transferred across national boundaries to meet seasonal needs. To the degree that this could be achieved without exploitation, without creating a paternalistic situation, people would gain in mutual understanding and good will.

Such fears and lack of faith, such anxiety-borne aggression and attempts at self-sufficiency, such competitive attitudes as have been described, will eat the vitals of the fairest international organization that can be established. Only as people address themselves to the problem of attitudes can they hope to find security. This does not mean that, because the task of revolutionizing attitudes is so immense, men must throw up their hands in despair. The assurance of economic stability, the relief of suppressed peoples and the institution of international machinery which will minimize war are necessary and possible first steps. To the extent that they reduce fear, repression and destruction, they will reduce the intensity of those emotions which develop unwholesome attitudes; they make re-education more practicable. The acute spasm must be relieved before the cure can be effected. Everyone raised above a level of deficient diet, everyone assured of an opportunity to earn his living, everyone recognized by his associates for his own skill or capacity or humanity, everyone accepted as an equal though he be white, black, yellow, red or brown, everyone saved from domination and from war, is someone whom it is more possible to reach with the gospel of democratic brotherhood.

In dealing with the barriers between nations, the time has come when reconsideration must be given to the whole problem of the small nation. In the world of *Realpolitik* there was reason for maintaining them as buffer states, as possible no-man's-lands between powerful states. The airplane and the panzer division, the speedup of mechanized armies and the meaninglessness of a few hundred miles to modern warfare make it possible to reconsider those small political units on their own merits. They are no longer useful as buffers and are of lessening importance as military allies. We can judge of them better now as cultural and economic units rather than as a screen of pawns to be manipulated in the interests of the great powers.

Throughout history, little nations have been unable to compete with larger political units in the highly competitive field of international politics. As military powers they have been insecure; economically they have generally been backward. The political independence of the Netherlands and the security of the Dutch Empire rested on the strength of the British Navy. When that failed, Holland and her colonial possessions fell. The independence of Belgium was as strong as the French Army. When that was liquidated, Belgian independence was over. The economic strength of Belgium and the Netherlands was established by the exploitation of even weaker people. The Balkans, freed from the suzerainty of the Ottoman Empire, became a whirlpool of currents in conflict and a bargain counter (and not a one-price counter at that) for competitive purchase by the greater powers. The more the Balkans struggled for a union or an entente, the higher the price paid by other powers to keep them in tutelage. Germany, Great Britain and France vied with each other to keep one or another of the Balkan countries on their pay rolls. The United States has substituted expensive pay-roll systems for the extravagant occupation method in parts of Latin America.

What security the small nations had was the result not so much of their own strength as of the indifference of the powerful and of the British policy of maintaining a balance of power, the Pax Britannica, that child of the pound Sterling and the Grand Fleet. For the greatest strength of the small nations was nothing but a passionate parochialism which survived centuries of oppression but proved politically and economically sterile whenever those nations received confirmation and were declared members of the community of nations.

This should not seem strange to us if we picture what the situation would be if the component parts of the great nations were broken up into their original units. Suppose France were again to become a group of states bounded as were the feudal states of Burgundy, Britanny, Normandy, Provence, etc. Or suppose that Great Britain were once more to be the separate kingdoms of England, Scotland and Wales. Suppose there were no union between the states which form the United States. Suppose again that the Union of Socialist Soviet Republics should be divided into separate republics. What a multiplicity of little lands there would be, militarily weak and economically inadequate! It is not difficult to recall Germany before Bismarck, and

Italy before Cavour, or feudal Japan before the end of the *shogunate*. If the historic boundaries of the parts that now are included in these great nations were tariff barriers and their farm fences were the barbed-wire entanglements of armies, could we expect an international organization much different from the medieval? Could we have realized the industrial development of today? We must always recall that the powerful nations are themselves unions or federations of once local states which preened their sovereign rights and were uneasy in the insecurity of their sovereign powers. Even today the constituent parts have not forgotten all of their provincial patterns. We must recall that in these great states, conflicts are for the most part resolved without violence, conflicts which the unassembled would have met with aggressive wars.

Independence or national sovereignty can become a shibboleth, an empty phrase of hysteria, if a factual basis of independence and sovereignty is not established, if there is little capacity for maintaining the welfare of the inhabitants and little power to assure security from foreign exploitation. This is so whether one is treating of established national units or people seeking "self-determination." The limits to Balkan self-determination are set by the degree of aggressiveness of the great nations of Europe; and the benefits of Balkan self-determination are measurable by their price in the balance-of-power market. And the same thing is in substance true of the Lowlands. It was their gold and their industrial development that gave them a higher price and greater dignity so that the powers had to tip their hats and call them "Mister" in greeting them.

The Scandinavian nations also could claim a perilous

independence. Geography helped them, and before the age of air power the British fleet was a threat to any imperialist design on them. What price self-determination for little Finland in the face of the Russian invasion of 1939 and German infiltration ever since! What European forces did not play a part in the overthrow of republican Spain? Czechoslovakia was the gold ring of the merry-go-round, with Germany, Poland and Hungary grabbing for it. Poland itself, for all its centuries of irredentism, for all the passion of its patriotism and for all its rich resources, was the prize grab-bag of all.

Where is the independence of Burma? In Thailand a corrupt ruling clique attempted to appease Japan when the benevolent patronage of France and Britain lagged; and Japan, which needed Thailand more than the European nations did, took over the country. How much self-determination did the land of Hailie Selassie possess without the arms of Great Britain, and, after its conquest by Italy, until the arms of Great Britain were ready for action? Can anyone doubt that if it had suited his needs Hitler would and could have overrun Sweden and Switzerland?

It is no recent development that small nations have stuck in the gorge of power politics. The proud and cultured city-states of Greece lost independence to each other and finally were the prey of Macedon. Read the story of the Kingdom of David, of the Kingdoms of Israel and Judah. Read of the invasions, the subjugations, the dispersals that they suffered.

Is it not plain that the little nation has the power, and not always even that power, to determine for itself of whom it will ask support and to whom it will pay the price of that support, but no independence to stand alone? Is it not plain, too, that the merging of "sovereign rights" is essential to obtain any freedom at all? This is what kingdoms such as Prussia and Bavaria, duchies such as Britanny and Burgundy, commonwealths and colonies such as Massachusetts and Pennsylvania, have done. They united or they federated.

It is not solely man-power for military machines which small states lack, but also economic wealth, natural resources and human resources which are necessary not only to back modern military machines but also to afford stability to peacetime industrial production of consumer goods.

Benes writes:

> Postwar planned economy will develop best in wider frameworks than are represented by the territories of small states. The economic sovereignty of states must be limited after the war, just as their political sovereignty must be—in Europe generally and in Central Europe particularly.

For the small state to subsist, it must give up ancient prerogatives of sovereign bodies—prerogatives frequently more fanciful than factual—in return for co-operative privileges in federations with other states. This is the meaning of the treaty made January 23, 1942, between the exiled governments of Czechoslovakia and Poland.

This is why the romantic notion of irredentist Zionism which has survived the centuries, runs counter to the needs of world security. In demanding a Jewish commonwealth it is seeking the organization of a new little national state.

Only on the basis of a Jewish commonwealth federated with the surrounding Arab states or a system of Jewish and Arab cantons in Palestine can there be an adequate basis for economic development and peace in Syria, Palestine, Iraq, Trans-Jordan and the Arabian Peninsula. A Jewish nation with a deficit economy, too feeble industrially and too small in population to defend its borders, will become a nation soliciting intervention, bargaining for support and in a state of friction with its neighbors. It will become the Albania of the Middle East. It will thus not even offer hospitality for cultural progress and spiritual expansion. It will either be the object of the paternalism of a great power or an armed stockade between the desert and the sea.

The price of liberty is more than eternal vigilance. It involves neighborly collaboration. But this has not been the way of nationalism. Of course the small nation has had some liberty of contract, the same liberty the weak have always had to contract with the powerful and the aggressive. But such engagements lack the substance of mutual respect for the dignity of the parties and of reciprocal development. The supercharged emotions of nationalism and irredentism have been the fruit of insecurity and the seed of aggression—and insecurity and aggression have been anathema to the development of democracy. It is not the white heat of nationalism which has developed democratic attitudes and institutions. This heat turned the democracy of the French Revolution into the dictatorship of Napoleon. It made of Poland between the world wars as undemocratic a nation as existed in Europe. It was the accompaniment to the imperialist melodies of the great nations—the most shameful dramas of democracies.

The dread of being minorities, the fear of being treated as younger brothers without a portion, is an important motivation to seek nationhood. The federation of small and insecure nations will inevitably lessen the problems of minorities. There is no minority problem for Scotsmen in London or Yorkshiremen in Wales. A Negro nation on the shores of the Caribbean would not solve the problem of the Negro minority in the United States. To the extent that anxiety on the part of a dominant group has induced aggression by it, the problem of minorities exists and will continue while such anxieties exist. Differences in language and color and faith and politico-economic ideology breed anxieties between peoples. This is particularly the case where people who are different from one another have no common opportunity for action on common interests. Federation in the interest of defense or economic welfare or cultural development affords such an opportunity. It is not through paternalism or competition but by the collaboration of equals that anxieties are quieted.

Insofar as federation reduces anxiety, it will, therefore, ease the situation of minorities. Insofar as federation makes for co-operative effort, it will diminish the chances for playing majorities and minorities off against one another in the power struggle. It will provide the means to a positive approach to mutual problems. When men work and play together they are less likely to eye one another with suspicion or to plot how to take advantage of each other than when they deal at arm's length or do not deal at all. Could it be doubted that the presence of Hungary in a

Balkan federation would mean better treatment of Transylvanians within the borders of Rumania and of Rumanians in Hungary? Were Greece and Bulgaria joined to work out common problems, is there any question but that each would deal better with people of the other? The economic and security benefits would help all alike; the home-country would represent the interests of people of similar national or religious origin living under other flags in the federation; and the spirit of co-operation would tend to carry over to other situations a recognition of the dignity of people who were different. As minority problems generally improved, that of the Jews would be eased, just as it has in the United States and Switzerland—and for that matter in Germany and Italy before the leaders of those lands offered racism as a balm to the insecurity of their nationals.

The failure to achieve the protection of minorities after the first World War was due to the failure to distinguish between law and life, between contract and action. Minority rights, like all other rights, can only be assured in one of two ways: by enforcement, which implies the ability and readiness to use force, or through co-operative effort, which means the acceptance of democratic attitudes and liberation from those fears caused by the existence of variations among people. In the long run only the latter means can assure the equal treatment of minorities. This is so because the nature of power is to corrupt the holder of that power, so that what commences as a weapon for liberty becomes in time a chain on the *status quo*. The power to guarantee minority rights is also power to impose or maintain selfish advantages. That is one reason why outsiders look with dread upon intervention by others and why majorities resent intervention. Certainly no one used force in the interest of minorities whose rights were guaranteed at Versailles until Hitler on the road of German chauvinism moved to "liberate" the Sudetenland and Danzig.

But, though there are still local and particular exceptions, the trend in democratic lands has been to grant equal rights to minorities. It is what one would expect as peoples get a sense of the strength to be found in their own integrity, in their growing independence of domination.

Benes, in a discussion of *The Organization of Postwar Europe*, emphasizes human rights over political rights.

> The protection of minorities in the future should consist primarily in the defense of human democratic rights and not of national rights. Minorities in individual states must never again be given the character of internationally recognized political and legal units, with the possibility of again becoming sources of disturbance. On the other hand, it is necessary to facilitate emigration from one state to another, so that if national minorities do not want to live in a foreign state they may gradually unite with their own people in neighboring states.

In other words, whether viewed from their own standpoint or from that of their fellows in other lands or from that of the majority, minorities tend to become focal points of aggression where they are not accepted or do not accept themselves as a part of their community. We come back then to the fundamental elements of democracy, the acceptance of variation and of co-operative development in the interest of the realization of individual human dignity. It is only as we can develop the acceptance of democratic attitudes that we can hope to eliminate minority problems. A bill of rights is as broad as its acceptance.

Instead of grandiose schemes for world organizations based on the model of the constitutions of the United States or the Soviet Union or the British Commonwealth, the nations would do well to expand already familiar and successful patterns of international co-operation. The possibilities of a more powerful International Labor Office have already been touched upon. The International Telegraph Union, the Universal Postal Union, the Interternational Bureau of Weights and Measures and the International Copyright Union have long histories of successful treatment of problems between nations. The facts that their governing bodies meet regularly, that they have permanent bureaus and that they address themselves to practical problems rather than ideological debates and maneuvers for power, give such organizations their opportunity for achieving tangible results. They are patterns for the successful handling of international affairs without supergovernment. Their methods and organization might well be considered in other fields. Nations, like men, can work together for limited objectives though their views of life and their general approach to each other may be quite different. The individualistic American farmer, for example, has been willing to help his neighbor raise his barn without feeling that either he or his neighbor had surrendered one jot of his rights or individuality.

Furthermore, there is ample precedent for the surrender

even of sovereign powers to such international bodies for specific purposes. Thus, in 1902, the Sugar Commission was formed to abolish export bounties and to limit import duties on sugar. This Commission was empowered by the member states to make "findings of fact" on the basis of which they bound themselves to alter tariffs. The Danube Commission also involved a surrender of sovereignty. It had the power to pronounce policies concerning the use of the Danube River, to establish dues, engage in construction and conduct trials of persons who violated its rules. This successful attempt at international co-operation and order was accomplished in one of the stormiest and most unstable regions of the world.

These are examples of voluntary surrenders of power in the interest of order and a co-operative approach to specific needs. Attitudes of paternalism and aggression were shed, and a fraternal attitude substituted. Furthermore, it is to be noted that all of these unions depend primarily on good will and the confidence of equals in one another, rather than on force and police powers. In other words, just as the co-operative and labor unions have afforded men and women a creative approach to democratic controls in domestic affairs, so those international institutions have offered a constructive approach on an equalitarian basis in the affairs of nations.

This does not mean that an international co-operative or labor movement cannot also be effective in international affairs. To the contrary, as international movements they offer the best possible opportunity for educating large masses of people to the integrity and basic similarity of peoples who differ from them. The extension of the activities of the International Labor Office and its recognition by governments which undertake to enforce its decisions could become a substantial means of international collaboration. This is practicable because that body will deal with real and common problems and because it could have the support of working people and employers whom it is set up to represent. Because it would deal with practical problems, it could be more effective as a binding force than the doctrinaire First and Second Socialist Internationals have been. Because it would deal with the lives of men and women rather than with political domination, it would be a more effective means of peace than the aggressive Communist Internationals. Because it would not be inhibited by the niceties of the balance of power, it could bind peoples together in a way that is impossible by treaties sealed with great seals and signed with flourishes of pens and trumpets.

Co-operatives, too, offer to cement people together. The similarity of consumer interests and the common needs of producers throughout the world have a binding force if national lines are not invoked to create competition.

In these tried institutions—co-operatives, labor unions, the International Labor Office, the Danube Commission, the International Telegraph Union, and the like—we have functional points of departure for international organization. It is only through developing from a functional basis that we can build firmly and democratically, that we can hope to enlist a broad base of support. For when political organization is put first, it comes first; and the emphasis falls on *Realpolitik, Macht, La Gloire,* balances of power and common political finagling dressed in the striped trousers and gray spats of diplomacy.

Moreover, if we think in terms of getting together on specific problems, we are more likely to face the irritations between neighbors and less likely to avoid them and permit them to fester while we search for solutions of matters halfway across the world. "Distrust those cosmopolitans who search out remote duties in their books and neglect those that lie nearest. Such philosophers will love the Tartars to avoid loving their neighbor," Rousseau wrote in *Emile*. If world-wide tariff questions cannot be settled without disturbing internal price structures and standards of living, at least tariff unions can throw down some barriers, enlarge economic units and give more people common interests. If world-wide questions of migration cannot be solved, at least regional solutions may be found. If people of different color or linguistic stock cannot lay aside at once their anxious antipathies, they can at least participate with their neighbors to supplement each other's natural wealth and human deficiencies. If world-wide disarmament arouses at this time too many fears that nations will be defenseless against rape by other nations, at least troops and forts can be removed from some borders as they have been for more than a century from that which divides Canada from the United States. Each such step is progress because it builds on collaboration rather than upon anxiety, and also because it can be brought closer to the people as a whole than can the acts of a super-government and its supernumerary police. Better one partnership, even in a limited enterprise, than a thousand nonaggression pacts and ten thousand police.

Throughout the centuries intellectuals have slept and

dreamed that words ruled the world. When men of action with motives of their own have cited texts in their struggle for power, intellectuals have been convinced that their dreams were realities, that somehow words, divorced from the men who heard or read or sang or bandied them, were power. So, having learned that there can be no "rights" without "sanctions," and no international "law" without a parliament, a court, a police and the other accoutrements of the state, the intellectual drive is for a new League of Nations, "self-implemented." Here are phrases of political science, of statecraft in place of poetry and religion, to bring quiet to the world.

This, of course, ignores the question of who is to make this international law and the attitudes of those who are to direct the international police. A police force is only neutral if the people who give it economic or ideological motivation are neutral. And positive law, the law of government, is man-made, not of mystical origin, and therefore subject to all the motivations and drives which cause men to act. We cannot, therefore, expect an international police force to be neutral—that is, to act impartially to keep the peace—unless we are certain that the nations which will control such a police force will not employ it for selfish ends—to attain domination over others, for example, or to impose a political, economic or other creed upon reluctant proselytes.

So once more, we find no solution to the problems of the world by expressing them in terms of organization if we ignore the frame of attitudes in which they are to function. The democratic world would not doubt the malevolence of an international government founded on the notion of

Aryan supremacy or the concept that the Japanese are a people chosen of the sun goddess to have dominion. Most people would object to the control of international organization by a godless dictatorship of the proletariat—or for that matter by a new Holy Alliance of an imperialistic white race or English-speaking union. In other word, if by any formula police and courts and legislative bodies and administrative bureaus are to play a paternalistic role, they will become institutions of oppression and they will retard democratic growth.

Let it be clearly understood that I make no suggestion that force can be eliminated from a world in which the aggressive spirit lives. The point is that transferring force from individual nations and alliances to a supergovernment will not destroy the attitude of aggression or assure us that force will not be employed in an aggressive spirit. Nor can force become disinterested by the establishment of a motley police of all nations, faiths and races. The mercenary Swiss Guards fought for the interests of French kings and the Papal States alike. The Empires of Rome and Britain and France were maintained by troops from Europe and Asia and Africa, black and brown and yellow and white troops.

What matters is the policy, the ideology, the attitudes behind the show of force. Therefore, no League of Nations and no implemented international law can bring security and well-being unless it consciously addresses itself to an educational program which will develop co-operative rather than aggressive attitudes and institutions.

The League of Nations established at Versailles failed, not because it had no effective military sanctions, not because the United States failed to join, but because, with the possible exception of the Soviet Union and some of the smaller nations, it was used as a lobby or hiring hall for the winning of allies and became a field for the maneuvering and balancing of power. The predominant theme of the League of Nations was not a co-operative effort of nations to deal together as equals for their mutual well-being, but a cynical assumption that there would be a new major war and that political alliances must be kept clear for military collaboration.

This was the dirty work of foreign offices. Nevertheless, ignoring the whole subject of attitudes, advocates of a new world or European federation propose again representation by states rather than popular representation. Thus in a scholarly article in the February, 1942, *Harvard Law Review*, Arnold Brecht writes:

> Such popular representation might easily lead not only to votes in conflict with the country's governmental policy but also to such a split in a country's votes as to annul its influence completely in important fields. Therefore a more realistic plan might envisage composing the legislative body of representatives who act and vote under the direction of their respective governments, as in the League of Nations.

This points up the concept that a government is divisible from its people and accepts without contest the fact that such a division exists. It assumes the paternalistic position that a foreign office knows best. It is based on the Hegelian principle that the state represents a "common will," which is something different from the sum of the people and their interests, that principle which finds its logical conclusion in totalitarianism and makes it hard for minds infected with philosophy of the Kant-Fichte-Hegel-Marx virus to accept the implications of democracy. It is only if federations or leagues are regarded as places for the exhibition of prestige and the teaming up of power combinations, that it can be of any importance if there is such "a split in a country's votes as to annul its influence." It is only if one accepts the fiction of man against society, of states being separate from and superior to the people, that votes of individual representatives can be deemed in conflict with national policy. In fact, this separation of people and state can only occur to the degree that the state is a bureaucracy and not responsive to the interests of the people.

As it does not appear likely that at the end of the second World War much of the world will be organized so that in each state the people can select popular representatives to a world league or federation, it scarcely seems worth while forming a supergovernment or chessboard to represent foreign offices. It will be far better to encourage regional federations, to expand the realm and power of the International Labor Office, to create a similar body in the interest of the world wide consumer and producer co-operative organization, and found an international education office to devote itself to experiment, training and the diffusion of educational techniques for the modification of attitudes.

This is not to say that any world federation or any league of nations would be worthless. Nor is it intended to suggest that all international force must be evil—or that we can live as if evil force, aggression, will not exist. What is intended and what is apparent is that federations and leagues with power of law enforcement are sources of hope only if their ends are moral and their attitudes not paternalistic. Only when and as nations join together as collaborators to meet their inevitable differences outside the frame of power conflict, only when force is utilized to disarm unruly aggressors—as a warden might disarm a maniac and not for personal aggrandizement or to feed sadistic needs—only then can world federations or leagues assure peace and well-being.

The first step is to clarify our ends; the second to modify our destructive and domineering attitudes. Now, in the midst of war have the United Nations more than superficial ends in common? Have they, any more than the Axis powers, common aims and interests beyond the winning of the war and the reduction of the enemy to impotence? With the defeat of the Axis, the United Nations will, if anything, be further apart. So long as their ends deny equality and respect for individual integrity no matter what the individual's race, creed, color or previous economic condition there will be paternalism and a process of jockeying for power.

Instead of pinning false hopes to a second-hand league of nations, instead of relying on the nervously grasped club of a police that will have various instructions from uncertain bosses, it will be better for the nations to move slowly, to progress along lines of functional collaboration until the time when common ends will be sought as well as spoken and the attitudes of men have been made clear and modified. That day will not come of itself but through education—through an education which will be more interested in the psychology and emotions of men than any education we have yet known. The task of such education will be the propagation of the democratic faith to free men of paternalism and make possible the acceptance of fraternity.

Part III

THE PROPAGATION OF THE FAITH

8

Plato's Sea Captain and Buddha's Navel

WHAT KIND OF EDUCATION will free men from paternalism and make possible the acceptance of fraternity? Will the propagation of the faith be achieved through the traditional liberal arts college and the traditional high schools of classical attitude as they existed before this second World War? Let us see.

In Book I of *The Laws,* Plato writes:

> We call one man educated and another uneducated although the uneducated man may sometimes be very well educated indeed in the calling of a sea captain or of a trader or the like. But we are not speaking of education in that narrow sense. We are speaking of that other education which makes a man eagerly pursue the ideal perfection of citizenship.

This passage is cited not as authority but because it illustrates two relevant phases and objectives of education and also because it presents the classical viewpoint of schoolmen who, in large measure, through the ages, have regarded trade-education to be education in a "narrow sense."

The words quoted have vitality, and they might have been written not by Plato twenty-four centuries ago in Greece, but by Thomas Aquinas in the thirteenth century Papal States or by university classicists the world over, today. For they all hallow a "higher education" leading to an "ideal perfection" while throwing a mere bone of condescension to popular education in the vocational field. This is not alone a matter of emphasis, nor would it be either fair or an answer to accuse these men of learning of being intellectual snobs. Rather, we are presented with fundamental concepts of living and of social relationships; and we must inquire not only into these concepts but into their relevancy and validity in the world in which we are now living.

The growing emphasis on vocational education is not an attempt to liquidate classical learning nor a surrender to inferior minds and standards. It is as inevitable today as are the spread of sanitation and electrification. For vocational education is indigenous to life among mechanisms and gadgets, just as schooling in the scientific method must be a part of education in a world recently turned topsy-turvy every half-generation by the findings of the laboratory. Pupils and students who are verbal-minded and possess a ready capacity to comprehend language symbols can absorb more of the classics as a part of their study of our cultural background than can most students. Those who can think in the symbolism of science can be better trained in the logic of scientific method than the majority of people. But whether verbal-minded, scientific-minded, clerical-minded, manual-minded, or with very little mind at all, everyone requires the attainment of some skill which will make him and her able to earn a living.

Any education which ignores this factor delays the maturity of the students because it permits them to evade facing what adult life will require of them as creative economic units. Any educational system which fails to arouse in young people a sense of a genuine relationship between what they study and adult enterprise must bring about a conflict in the student which will make school work seem like a childhood game which cannot illuminate labor and is irrelevant to its ends.

Such skill, whether verbal or manual, whether predominantly intellectual or physical, cannot readily be picked up today; it is rarely passed on from father to son. Of course, ability to earn a living and capacity for a given vocation are by no means surety of employment. The fact that young people are made more employable does not in any great measure make jobs where the economy of the world does not otherwise provide the incentive or means to create employment. But the possession of skill is essential, not only as a means to bread and shelter and greater stability in job holding, but also to the achievement of that sense of capacity which raises the self-esteem and stabilizes the character of people. These are the aims of vocational instruction. To deny them a place in the scheme of education, and a respected place, is to live among shadows, beautiful perhaps, but certainly silent shadows. Some day the schools and colleges will recognize that all students are entitled not only to acquaintance with their cultural background, but to vocational skills—each in accordance with and to the extent of his capacities, whether they be hand, head or machine skills, highly specialized or more general. Such recognition should come because cultural background without vocational interest and skill is inevitably sterile; and vocational skill without some understanding of the relations of things and people is invariably servile.

Let us consider again the quotation from Plato.

Why is the student of symbols—that is, the reader—deemed educated and the man "very well educated indeed" in a calling or trade requiring skill of the hand and eye and decisive judgment deemed uneducated? Why should it be assumed that the sea captain with the education of his calling and the trader with the education of his trade would not "eagerly pursue the ideal perfection of citizenship"?

In the Athens of Plato, traders and artisans, even the great sculptors, did not share in the citizenship of the city. Farmers might be citizens, but by the Periclean Age many of them had become gentlemen farmers. The sea captain and the trader were foreigners, the cobbler and the artisan slaves. The land and the capital, the leisure and the intellectual life were Greek. The higher learning and the eagerness to pursue the ideal perfection of citizenship were only to be achieved by those legally entitled to citizenship. Here was an aristocracy, membership in which entitled one to the arms of war and a passport to contemplation. It is worth noting that all of the Aristotelian discussions of autocracy and democracy dealt with political forms within the confines of this group, the particular structure of Greek government in each instance being, as Aristotle pointed out, that which was appropriate to the needs of the group in power. It was consequently inevitable that sea captain and trader should not be deemed educated in a democracy which was democratic only within the confines of an hereditary class and in which social practice severed on class lines those who might labor from those who might think and rule, who might pursue the perfection of citizenship. And where, as in the case of Plato and those in his tradition, it was not functional effectiveness and satisfaction that was sought, but the ideal perfection of citizenship or of beauty or of something else, it was inevitable that contemplation should have risen from reality, should have left earthiness for fantasy. When the first great rush of abstract thinking was over, after Aristotle had summed up all that was known of man and nature (perhaps all that could be known without the willingness of thinkers to make manual effort), it followed that thought was devoted to piling untried fantasy on untried fantasy until its heights were reached in realms of mysticism.

The ideal perfection of citizenship, which had at least a class basis in Plato, became in Plotinus a perfection to be achieved through contemplation of the Good, and in early Christian thought, by way of Plotinus, into a faith in God and participation in the congregation of Christendom where for centuries education was something for the clergy and the court only. Here were the elect of the elect—for only those of the faith had grace, all others being infidels or heretics and thus ineligible to citizenship in the City of God. The great mass of believers were offered such education as was thought necessary to give them that faith which would cause them eagerly to pursue the ideal perfection of citizenship in the City of God. Their trades they learned from their fathers or as apprentices. Those who ruled the elect from altar and throne were taught to read and figure and sing.

Among the Jewish people, too, the man of the soil was looked down upon as ignorant and unreliable; and his problems, his interests and those of tradesman and artisan, except insofar as they presented ethical considerations, were not the problems and interests of the schools. As the result of continual annotation and discussion, Talmud and Cabbala became balloons of mental play, the possession of a specialized group.

With the fall of the Moorish Empire in Spain and the destruction of its schools, roughly the same thing occurred to Moslem education, which buried itself in the Mosque. And among the Hindus one finds the classic example of culture and education which disregarded the common things in common lives for the "higher" things of ideals and perfections and classical interests. A caste of untouchables must lead to a Buddha contemplating his navel.

For so long a period had the Middle Ages consumed the classics cooked in the wine of theology, and so thoroughly had they digested these classics, that it came as a shock in the twelfth and thirteenth centuries to meet the animal face to face, actually to read the original Aristotle. Classical knowledge and thought had burst through the web of marginal notes, glosses and palimpsest which had buried them. They cried, "Fraud" and "Garble!" When confronted with the works of a philosopher who had used his eyes, the scholars annotating and disputing and the Buddhas contemplating and contemplating, were in danger of becoming intellectual Tibetan lamas, searching "ideal perfection" in fantastic isolation. It was the genius of Thomas Aquinas for Christendom and Maimonides for the Jews to feel this crisis and to resolve it by reconciling the rediscovered wisdom of the ancient world with the basic ideologies of their own world. Here were triumphs of synthesis which in themselves became classics to be thumbed over, annotated, becommentaried and befootnoted until the contemplating latter-day Buddhas beatified them in doctors' dissertations. For a moment Buddha raised his eyes from his navel and created new classics, but he never saw the sea captain or the trader.

I am not suggesting that the classics or the civilization of former ages are not worthy of study. On the contrary, they may be useful to an understanding of the emotional background to problems of the day and an illumination of the things which men have sought or which they feared. The study of the Latin language can be an aid to the appreciation and mastery of the English language. Plato, Aristotle and sacred writings can be stimulants of thinking and emotion and guides to the understanding of otherwise incomplete pictures of centuries in which many of our present attitudes found early expression. The myths repeated by Homer and the primitive practices reported by Livy and Tacitus may throw light upon submerged psychological relationships of men today. The experienced wisdom of the practitioners who wrote Justinian's Code and of Machiavelli may be applicable to modern problems, not because the problems themselves are even similar but because the patterns of power politics and human psychology are basic to all ages. An understanding of Bacon and Descartes, of Locke and Spinoza, may explain the thinking of succeeding generations—if, and the if is important, if their generation and succeeding generations are studied as living, bread-earning, lusty and anxious people seeking not ideologies or philosophies except incidentally to obtaining satisfactions and to the shedding of guilt feelings.

In primitive society art was not art for its own sake, but in the interests of totemism. Its end was to obtain power over, or the protection of, or to participate in the being of the totem animal or, later, of a departed spirit. Custom was not pursued merely because it was disagreeable to change, but as a ritualistic experience of totem or taboo. Thought was not an end in itself, but a prelude to action. It took civilization to raise the pattern of neuroses to a virtue for normal men, to make thought worlds real worlds, to pursue the ideal of perfection. And it took civilization to transfer from totem and departed spirit to classic and departed sage its conflicting emotions of love and hate, fear and satisfaction. When the new god, the new ideology, seems to fail, there is again the longing for the golden calf —the old totem and classics. Departed spirit and sage appear to possess a power which living and familiar persons lack.

It was not the attitude of classical contemplation, but a mood of dynamic inquiry as to how the needs of men were to be met and the limits of man's world, that set into motion science and thought in the days of Copernicus and Galileo, just as it had set into motion the arts, the inquiries, the political and commercial adventures of the Greek era. Buddha might not be interested in the nature of the navel he was contemplating, or as to the nature of himself and the phenomenon of his contemplation. But others were. These were men who were not content only to think; they examined themselves and others, studied the technique of thinking and what lay behind it physiologically and anthropologically, guessed at generalizations and tested and retested these. They were interested in the ways of the sea captains, in their skills as well as their voyages and cargoes; they accepted the trader—perhaps because the trader was taking over some of the power that had resided in the church and court. Sovereignty placed its powers behind the "law merchant," and science made itself of service to commerce and later to industry. In the seventeenth, eighteenth and nineteenth centuries, men educated only in "that narrow sense" took over the greater part of the earth, developed it, created knowledge and spread it as the classicists had never been capable of doing.

Of course, the schools did not offer "education in that narrow sense." It took centuries to bring about the teaching of post-Aristotelian science, more centuries to introduce laboratory science; and only in our day has education for a vocation been introduced below the college level (and there except for medicine it has been largely in the classical professions of lawyer, teacher and clergyman). It is only recently that universities and secondary schools have ceased to be institutions for the select few, that the sons and daughters of sea captains and traders, and that future mariners and grocery clerks have been able to enter such schools. It is only recently that the base of power has been broadened, that workers through their organizations have begun to achieve equality in their dealings with those powerful interests which have been the employers of the men with academic learning.

In western Europe, in the United States, in the British Commonwealth, in a few other lands, education has been broadening its base to include every child through childhood—and this means children and young people of every capacity and interest, every economic group and family educational background. Neither the Athenian citizen nor the medieval churchman was concerned with education of such catholicity. Yet this very broadening of the educational base, this expansion of opportunity for schooling (and the concurrent enlargement of scope and diversification of program) is the brightest and most dynamic part of the ideology of democracy. We go to extraordinary effort and considerable expense to develop the capacities of mentally and physically handicapped children; classic Sparta left them in the mountains to die. We take artisans into high places in our government and make men of humble origin chief men in our states; classic Attica kept them as slaves or otherwise denied them citizenship. We cultivate the silliest little artistic talents for the joy and satisfaction and self-realization they may yield; in Greece they were little practiced by citizens and in some forms, notably architecture and drama, they were for millenia the monopoly of the state and the religious institutions.

The rapid expansion of cultural opportunity and the dynamic qualities of democracy and experimental science have inevitably diluted classical learning and altered the quality of liberal arts education through a dispersion of individual interest. Review courses and innumerable elective courses in the experimental and political sciences, in the fine arts and in vocational subjects, have taken places of equal rank with the liberal arts, have even replaced in greater measure the seven liberal arts which for about two thousand years were traditional: grammar, rhetoric, dialectic, arithmetic, geometry, music and astronomy. Logic as a tool has replaced logic as an end. As a tool it is important to experimental science; as an end it brought sterility to nineteenth-century Anglo-American common law as it had to twelfth-century scholasticism.

The question is, has this been a price worth paying? And this question can be disposed of only by considering a series of other questions. Do you accept democracy with its diffusion of educational opportunity or are you continually weeping for the lost virginity of your classicism? Do you regard education as a certificate of membership in a cult, a class, a caste, a secret society of elders and medicine men, or is education to you a means of developing individual potentialities and social intercourse on a better informed level? Do you seriously believe that scholarship and learning can long remain creative if limited in the scope of its content or the congregation of its participants?

Your classicist from Chicago or Oxford or Paris or anywhere else, with the categories of Aristotelian logic on his lips and the lays of ancient Athens in his heart, would make the classics the core of education. He would find a place for science, a lesser place; but to him the education of sea captain and trader is definitely education in a narrow sense, perhaps even in an unworthy sense. He shows little or no appreciation of the lessons of psychology concerning the process of learning. The classic theory of education approaches life by looking backwards. It would have us drive by looking into the mirror facing the rear of the car rather than through the windshield. Escaping from the microscopic attitude of statistical social science (which by all means should not be permitted to envelop one) the classicist would substitute the periscopic version. A neo-Platonist, he can point to Plato, who saw life as shadows of reality; but at least Plato believed that he could not find any greater reality except through contemplation. While purporting to be a follower of Aristotle, he does so through the reflective eyes of Saint Thomas, whereas Aristotle looked long on life and nature and established his universals on the basis of his own observations, not on shadows. Neither Plato nor Aristotle had the telescope at their disposal, nor the flexible powers of electricity at hand. If they had had, it is not impossible that they would have viewed the universe differently, that the Greek tradition of social respectability which left handicrafts to slaves and *metics* would not have controlled them. No such excuse is available to modern educators, any more than it is to the British aristocracy, which has fed the young of its ruling group for centuries on classics and ruled with one eye on the feudal system.

It might be pointed out that one cannot long look on reflections and shadows as a way of viewing life without speedily seeing ghosts. Static primitive society and reactionary societies are governed by ghosts, by ancestral shades, but not progressive societies. Free of guilty feelings, they can accept and try to comprehend the past without the compulsion to propitiate or repeat it.

The climate of culture—the culture of time and space limitations—cannot be ignored. The classics may enliven the past and explain features of the present, but they are no map to the future. Emotional patterns are repetitive, but history does not repeat itself.

One of our modern scholastics makes the excellent point that most people do not know how to read. If they did, he argues, they could then read the classics, they could study with the great dead teachers instead of only learning from a rehash of the great in the classrooms of the ordinary. It is a good point that reading is at best not merely an ability to understand the words on a printed page; that a proper reading should develop an understanding of the purpose of the author, an appraisal of the success with which he achieves his purpose and a judgment as to the relevancy of the argument of the book in the light of the reader's other experience and knowledge. Good teachers have known this for a long time. Within the generation remedial reading techniques (and remedial arithmetic techniques, too) which diagnose and correct reading deficiencies have been developing. They have in large measure, though not entirely, been made necessary by the very circumstance of which complaint is made: that most students have not learned to read with understanding.

Why is this? I believe it is an outcropping from the democratization of education. Formerly student bodies were composed of people who *wanted* to go to school; now, in the primary years and more and more in the years of secondary schooling, young people *must* go to school. Wanting to learn rather than resisting learning makes learning easier and more certain. When the student body was small, it comprised principally the children of people who already had an educational background above the average. It was not the children of the illiterate and the semi-illiterate, not the children of the immigrant, the ditch-digger and the laundress who went to high school—and certainly not in droves to universities. It was the children, mostly the boys, of people who were well read or wealthy who finished high school and went to college.

Research has indicated that family educational background is at least one important factor affecting intelligence quotients—the measure of learning facility. So in former days a greater proportion of students were possessed of a background which fitted them for that kind of verbal education which was patterned for a high intelligence quotient. Moreover, compulsory school attendance laws have brought within the schoolhouse hundreds of thousands of dull-minded children who cannot be expected to read on a collegiate or even high school level, but who in a democracy are entitled, nevertheless, to such education as will develop their capacities. The schools have failed to meet their needs, because, in the academic tradition, they have placed these dull children year after year in unequal competition with brighter children. This hodge-podge of students also interfered with the learning progress of the brighter children. But in this we have only growing pains of democratic education which can readily be corrected by any society willing to pay the cost.

Though they may not be material for classical students, those dull but otherwise normal young people are educable, as anyone who has worked with them knows—that is to say, educable if one conceives of education as the development of individual capacities and opening the way to individual satisfactions and social co-operation. They would be unable to master the cornucopia of great books listed by Professor Adler; but the inversion of the cornucopia into a duncecap would scarcely answer the problems of democratic living.

As citizenship today is more inclusive than it was in the days of Plato, it is difficult to see how the state can exclude its duller members from educational opportunity unless it is also prepared to exclude them from full participation in citizenship. It might be unfair to accuse our classicists of any such intention, although many another has believed in educational tests for voters.

If the dull were to be deprived of their privileges as citizens, either because they were dull or because they failed to absorb that picture of the culture and institutions of the state which state narcissism desired to preserve, they would, with progressive rapidity, lose the competence to maintain themselves and to defend themselves and gradually be pushed into becoming a class of untouchables. For if there is anything to be learned from history of human institutions, it is that any group in a community deprived of rights or powers possessed by others becomes increasingly degraded and weakened, increasingly feared and hated, until it becomes more and more hateful, fearful and impotent even to itself. That is why the schooling of the dull members of a democracy must not be regarded as something less than education or even as a lesser or narrower education.

There is unquestionably a large part of all people who enjoy doing things with their hands; some of them dull, some normal, some among the most able and understanding. To them the satisfactions to be derived from observation and creation and even tinkering are at their best objectives as worthy as those of men and women who find their satisfaction in the observations of the inner eye and in tinkering with symbols. Not all men with skill of hand regard the use of such skill as a joy; it may be no more than the most practicable way to earn a livelihood. But even the man who sees in his vocational skill no more than something to be bartered for bread and butter, and who never heard of Plato and Aristotle or the president of his state university need not be ashamed. Who will believe that he is less worthy than the instructor who teaches by the clock or who offers in barter for a doctor's degree or professorship his routine vocational skill, devoted perhaps, to putting into book form some *ersatz* for original thinking or the doctored photograph of the ideas of bigger men? It is not skills or knowledge that are worthy or unworthy, but the uses to which men put them.

Consequently, as human enterprises develop our needs and new means for their satisfactions, the social studies and scientific and vocational education have entered the schools to challenge the monopoly held for so many centuries by the traditional liberal arts. The breakdown of this monopoly of educational content parallels (*ex post facto* it is true) the breakdown of the monopoly of social and political control by church and aristocracy and the monopoly of scientific knowledge by church and university—it parallels the division of labor, the disappearance of feudalism and the passing of static society.

Recent centuries have incorporated vast spheres in our knowledge and developed inventions which, in classical days, would have condemned the inventor to exile or unpleasant death as a magician; these are now accepted as a functional part of everyday living. These spheres of knowledge and these inventions arouse curiosity in our children. Seeing alone is not believing. They want to know how and why these wizardries occur; they want to try for themselves, and by trying they learn.

At the same time, doing things, trying things in school, is in part compensation for the lack of doing things and trying things in urbanized life. Mechanized homes, mechanized farms, mechanized transportation, mechanized entertainment have transformed our social ways more than we realize. Domestic skills have atrophied, household functions which had always placed responsibilities on the family and its members no longer exist. The janitor, the cannery, cheap factory-made clothing, the replacements to be obtained in the five and ten cent store for what is worn or broken, gas and electric stoves, mechanical refrigeration, installment buying and many other conveniences and facilities have taken from people activities and purposes which had been a normal or even necessary part of everyday life. Those activities and purposes in themselves had educational values. It is because these daily contacts with facts and skills and responsibilities have been so drastically reduced that facts and skills and responsibilities must find a larger sphere in the program of schools.

The old school could carry on a verbalistic program; it could limit its field principally to words with little danger of engendering a schism between the world of books and the world of experience which goes beyond books. Life outside the school, domestic and social life, supplied opportunities for translating school symbols in terms of sensory experiences. Political democracy was not threatened by the frustration of hundreds of thousands of young people from whom civilization has withdrawn creative opportunities at home and at times denied opportunity for work after graduation from school.

The modern school, on the other hand, must act in a world of more limited home experience, and it must teach the tool subjects (reading, writing and figuring) and the cultural heritage under the shadow of postgraduate frustration for a large part of its students. Therefore schools today must approach education differently from the old schools, differently even from the schools of half a generation ago, if they are to fulfill the needs of modern society. The war has increased the urgency of society's demand that schools recognize the work-a-day world and transfer their emphasis from symbols to experience. It has emphasized the need to understand man and his behavior—that is, his searches for satisfactions—more than to know his words and the history of his thoughts.

If the teacher has not been too narrowly educated in the classics, the sciences, the social sciences or even the more directly vocational subjects, if he has the teaching spark, will it matter in the long run where the point of departure may be? Electricity, the law of real property or the mercantile system may not afford identical ramifications, but they each offer avenues of culture to the teacher, who is not wedded to the "dead teachers" of his speciality; and they present a learning situation to the student whose mind is stimulated by the particular approach. But there is no deader dog than the mishandled classics, as generations of Latin students can attest; and there is no more vitiating intellectual effort than that which commences with a worship of past greatness and leads to regurgitative contemplation of ideas disrupted from the current of their context.

There is no progress in the Daughters-of-the-American-Revolution type of mind, a mind which finds its highest achievement in the misjudged deeds of its ancestors. Freud tells of the dispossessed sons who banded together to slay the father, devoured him to absorb his powers and generation after generation repeated the act symbolically through totem worship. In classicism there is much of totem worship, too much reliance on acquiring the powers of the departed through the consumption of their learning and the imitation of their art.

"Return to Aristotelian categories so nobly reinterpreted by Saint Thomas," cries the twentieth-century scholastic. "Come back again to Aristotelian logic," beseeches the neoclassicist. "Make these things cornerstones in education. Hear, all ye educators who are exalting the education of sea captain and trader and even hem-stitcher in his or her calling, hear ye! Return again to the well-worn golden calf of Nicomachea!" The gold of Aristotle is no less golden than it was; the polish that Saint Thomas put upon it is no less brilliant. But, bright or dull, this golden calf has no longer the same market. We cannot forget how categories and logic lacked fertility; that they terminated in the senseless brilliant disquisitions of scholasticism; that the scholarship of the medieval university was the story of Abelard and Héloïse, a love of the beautiful terminating in castration by the ancient.

Would it not be better to omit subjective or moral judgments altogether as to whether this or that education is or is not education in a "narrow sense" or in a broad sense and whether the citizenship which is to be pursued is an "ideal perfection" or just citizenship? As a matter of fact, this is precisely what the age of science and the democratic state and the democratization of education have accomplished—and it is this tendency toward detachment of educational criteria from subjective judgments expressed by moralistic adverbs and adjectives that the classicists fear. They want neither to surrender their subjective judgments nor to test moral judgments in situations of life—that is, by the development of children and the satisfaction of their needs.

To concede that education for the practical is not narrower or lower education, would be a concession that classical learning stands on a par with vocational training, consumer education or laboratory science; that the discussion of great books of science is not better than the use of the faculties of experience—the hand and the eye, the senses and the emotions. Experience has taught us that "beauty is truth, truth beauty" only in a subjective sense—that this is not all one needs to know—that "ideal perfections" are only subjective. For they are the fabric of ideas and aspirations which are not subject to scientific proof or observation. This does not mean that such ideas and aspirations, such equation of beauty to truth, are not valid as ennobling subjective experiences and as the material for achieving educational values. But just because they are subjective they are not criteria for forming educational judgments and controlling educational practices. Because your needs and your experiences differ from mine, your sense of beauty and mine will not be the same; and your ideal perfection and mine may differ. Consequently, in many things our truths will not prove to be identical.

If education is to be regarded as basic in a dynamic democracy, let us subject it not only to the test of the judgment of the past, but also to the criteria of its relevancy to the age of science. The age of science and the trend to democracy have given stature to objective judgments and to the common things in the lives of all people. You cannot fashion a democracy if the different interests of people are to be classified as broad or narrow, ideal or common; if the capacities of one group are to be satisfied and those of a less complex nature ignored. Who in a democracy could make such a classification? Would it not require a caste system which in itself would be a contradiction in modern democracy? It may be worth while for a democracy to pay highly for the training of a technical expert; but it need not therefore regard as less worth while the development of hundreds of untalented young people to perform unskilled tasks, to lead satisfactory lives, and to express with their fellows at the polls, on a less sophisticated level perhaps, but on an equality, their beliefs as to what is best for them and theirs.

Industrial and mechanical development, moreover, have opened more opportunities for men and women—not necessarily to fortune or power—but certainly in the multiplication of occupations, the expansion of leisure time, the transfer of accent from isolated farm to congested city. Modern commerce has stimulated the imagination and invoked new necessities through advertising and entertainment. From this development come needs and opportunities which are translated into demands for educational satisfactions that are not to be circumscribed by the needs of candidates for the ministry, the bar and the pharmacopoeia of medicine.

Indeed, the educational effects of a culture predicated upon propaganda to convince average and subaverage people that there are new and splendid necessities which they must obtain, and which is garnished by entertainment which flatters them with introductions to the fictional grandeurs of the screen and the periphery of the fine arts, cannot be too strongly underscored. And these commercial educational effects call in turn for schooling that is not divorced from them, which does not close its eyes to the educational processes of life beyond the schools. The products of mass production may not be works of art, and the entertainment of the masses may not be of classical standard—but there they are, plus the political power of millions to insist that the things they live by and enjoy shall be given respectability and vitality in their lives, that they shall be taught to use and appreciate them.

Moreover, an economic system, whatever it may be, requires not only skills for production but also adaptability in consumption. It is one of the tasks of schools (whether or not they are conscious of it) to develop those skills and foster such adaptability in the interest of maintaining a thriving economy. Thus the novelty of today must illuminate the lesson of tomorrow.

It is certain that all state-maintained schooling aims at education in the duties of citizenship as well as its privileges and the manner in which the former are to be performed and the latter realized. Every state seeks to assure its longevity by continuance of its ideals and customs. Propaganda of the political and economic faith of the dominant groups of the state (narrow groups in autocratic states, broader groups as democratization is realized) is the long-term technique to this end. And schooling set for such ideals and customs has come to be the primary long-term institution for this propaganda of faith. But with democracy has been introduced not merely a public school of a narcissistic culture seeking its political and economic immortality. In that school, perhaps because the interests of the dominant groups have expanded and concurrently the cultural narcissism has expanded, people have demanded to know not only the generalities of citizenship and the political and economic world, but specifically the realities of their own functioning in their own environment. Men and women in democratic lands have come to accept Jefferson's, not Plato's, objective of education: "To give to every citizen the information he needs for the transaction of his own business."

It is this impact of the scientific age, this humanism of democracy, that the classicist fails to appreciate. Like the scientist, he starts with the *a priori* idea, the feeling, the intuition; unlike the scientist, he embellishes it with some reason and more feeling but without objective valuation. He is sure of his criteria. Beauty tends to be truth to him absolutely, not in a relative sense, not as it springs from new experience or the satisfaction of individual impulses. Such absolutism was relevant to the work of Saint Thomas, who was demonstrating the philosophic validity of the authoritarian church. It is also relevant to categorical German philosophy and its Marxian offspring, which again are phrased in authoritarian idioms. But neither scientific nor democratic thinking can by their very nature be absolute. The one cannot evade exceptions which prove new rules, nor the other avoid variations inherent in mankind, and remain science or democracy.

Neither science nor democracy can find release in the paternal protection of certainties; but it is this very need for dependent thought and action, the search for protective certainty, which has thrown faltering peoples into the arms of dictators, has encouraged them to find in father-fantasies the hope of security. The intellectual phase of this neurosis is to be found in present-day classicism. For classicism that is unrelieved by objective experiment, thought that is unrelated to eye and hand, have become again and again through the years retreats for neurotic scholarship, escapes for him who sees daring in an asterisk and finds immortal security in a footnote.

The plea for the classics as the foundation of education is a plea for the certainties of the past, for certainties no longer convincing except as experience and experiment have proven them, and otherwise no longer relevant except as they evidence the unexpressed yearning for authoritarianism and all that implies.

The aesthetic qualities of some classics have value today. As the classics illuminate patterns of behavior and explain ideas, they have a continuing value. But neither the classical content nor the academic approach to education have been adequate to alter destructive attitudes. For every advance in freedom stimulated by classical example, there have been scores of such examples to hold men back from attaining freedom. It is not the classical heritage that will provide effective education for the propagation of the democratic faith. We must search further.

9

Man Cannot Live by Words Alone

THROUGHOUT THE STORY of democracy there has been a trend, fluctuating it is true, but a definite trend towards equalizing opportunity. To a great extent it has been through the schools that democratic people have attempted to bring about the process of equalization. This has been particularly true of schools in the United States. The function of these schools has been the extension of opportunities to everyone to recognize his abilities and to utilize the chances which society opens to him.

Even with all of our available knowledge, the school alone cannot equalize the mentalities of all children. It does not pretend to attempt it. The school cannot make the interests, the faculties and the facilities of all coincide, even were that desirable. The school cannot make everyone measure up to the same standards; nor can it be sufficiently sure and omniscient even to devise a standard as a goal for all. A fallacy of Nazism is the doctrine that the state can do this very thing, can establish universal standards of devotion and achievement—of course, only after destroying all dissident and differentiated groups. But this very necessity for eliminating such groups in order to bring about equalization is an admission by the Nazis of the failure of their own thesis. It is like a laboratory experiment in which all elements which might disprove an hypothesis are first carefully eliminated.

Variety is so much a part of life that no society can feel secure or be long effective which closes its eyes to the fact. Variation may not be the spice of life to Hitler, Stalin, Mussolini, Hirohito and Company, but they have had to pay the price of a great pay roll for gunmen and publicity agents because they dared not ignore it.

It must be borne in mind that variations in needs and choices occur not only among individuals, but also in time. What meets the needs of Abner Stout today may not meet the requirements of his son; and it is entirely possible that Abner's father on the farm had as a boy quite a different set of needs. If democratic schools are to respond to these varying needs, to use a cliché, education must concern itself with the whole student. By this, of course, we cannot mean with his entire life. The school cannot replace the family psychologically or economically, and it should not attempt to do so. Public education should not enter the emotion-laden field of religious education, unless the school is to be an agency of a state religion, which immediately denies equality to nonconformist religious groups, and thereby belies the equalitarian nature of democracy. With full consciousness that other agencies, social units and conditions are also affecting the lives of our pupils, the entity of the pupil with which education must be concerned involves the physical, the emotional, the social and the intellectual personality. These, of course, impinge upon one another and intermingle in their expression—which in complete development grows, through feeling and doing, to thought and experiment.

What, then, are the fields of action for an education whose concerns are to be so broad?

The method of human communication and thought is through symbols, through words and signs conveyed directly by the voice or the hand or some object, and indirectly by gestures, as in Hindu and Balinese dancing. It is essential, therefore, that we offer to all the opportunity to learn these methods of human communication and thought and, so far as the individual needs of the pupil require, something of the content of human communication and thought in the past. Consequently, a good education will teach the understanding of the symbols on the page—that is to say, the child must learn not only that he is looking at a sign which, when translated to speech sounds like *home*, but that sign and sound are referring to a real something in his life, a reality comprised of other persons, of furniture, of rest and food, of emotion and color and many other things.

We get so used to words that we sometimes forget they are not the real thing. We Americans think of ourselves as a practical nation—and indeed we can be. We can build great dams and power projects in our rivers, mechanize farming and invent the assembly line. But often we are the slaves of sweet slobber; we cause ourselves to serve in a veritable daisy-chain-gang. We assume that an idea caught in words is as good as realized—baptism in the Mississippi is itself salvation. Thus we can declare men equal, assume that they are equal and act in such a way as to deny equality. We gulp down advertising and other propaganda, but we distrust such education as may challenge our words or measure our ideas against our accomplishments or our slogans against documented facts. In this we are, of course, not unique. All men today are the heirs of men who trusted in magic, who believed that incantation could ward off evil and invoke good. So the power of the word has blinded men through the ages to the disparity between the word and other power lurking behind it.

One of our difficulties in education is that the writers of books and the teachers of children have themselves in many cases had little experience of the fact behind the word. Teachers and writers of textbooks for the most part merely reverse the role of student and teacher. After having been taught in normal school and college, they move to the front of the classroom and teach others what they have learned. They see the world as readers and tourists, not as participants. They cannot be expected to experience everything they teach about or write about, but one may suspect most of them are not conscious either of this lack in themselves or that they are teaching signs, not realities.

Moreover, the movement of civilization which gives meanings to words and slogans in one generation veils their sense to the next. The automobile has made quite meaningless to most of us the qualities of a team of horses or yoke of oxen, their care and harness and handling. The self-contained feudal manor which our children study in school cannot well be appreciated by a generation that buys everything in stores and makes few repairs at home.

Man Cannot Live by Words Alone

The superintendent of one of our city school systems recently asked an elementary class: "What is it that people sometimes have on their hands—and I don't mean fingernails." One child answered, "Troubles"; another said "Relatives." But the superintendent was thinking of something else; he was thinking of calluses which many of the children had never seen. The story is illuminating in that it reveals the change that city life and machine civilization have brought about—where calluses are not common for a large part of the population, certainly not for children who lack the experience and educational value of chores.

The school must teach not only the meaning of words and comprehension of what is read, but also the meaning of number symbols in such a way that the child will understand them as expressing the physical relations of things, not merely as numerical abstractions. We learn to brush our teeth because we also learn of dental decay, and if we are inclined to forget, most of us are effectively reminded by the buzz of the dentist's drill. But why should we have anything to do with numbers beyond learning to make change—that is, until we are old enough to know we want to be bookkeepers, accountants, mechanics or engineers?

As arithmetic is generally taught, there is little motivation to learn the numerical relations of things. Even after having humanized the teaching of arithmetic through the devices of multiplying dollars, distributing apples and making problems out of airplane speeds and batting averages, we have nevertheless generally missed the point. We have needled the draught, but it has not become champagne. For to most of us numbers speak as separate words, not as sentences. We are agonized in the face of a simple equation: it is as though numbers and forms were words without thought.

Finally, symbols must become a means of thinking; they must become tools of the thought process. The sentences we read must live as thoughts to be at times analyzed and applied to our own experience. "This is a cat" may find its place in a syllogism with "All cats tread softly."— "Now is the time for all good men to come to the aid of their party" is more than a practice sentence; it is a thought. Students must be stimulated to co-ordinate the facts for which the symbols stand and to discover further facts and to appraise them, and again to use the appropriate symbols. Here method becomes important. The co-ordination and discovery of facts, and the appraisal of results, can best be achieved through placing responsibility on the student, by having faith in the child. This can be done from nursery school to postgraduate education. Children probably pick up more errors from books handed to them and from well-intentioned dicta of their teachers than from the satisfaction of their own curiosity through inquiry and experiment.

This need not imply that, by placing responsibility on the child, the teacher is to be relieved of responsibility for guidance, stimulation or appraisal. The teacher must still arouse curiosity, guide the inquiry and experiment, and participate in the appraisal. The important thing is that the symbols men live by should be tools and themselves vital experiences which lead to further experience, not treasures to be hoarded, or screens to further vision, or opiates to independent thought and expression.

But symbols must be refreshed for each generation by contact with reality, unless they are to become shadows in the imagination, unless they are to become immaculate fantasies untouched by the sensory world, or simply to reproduce further ideas and emotions and feed on their offspring. Symbols must draw renewal and nutrition from experience. The tools of the mind must be kept keen and tempered by constant testing and use.

"Successive values, to be compared, must be represented; but the conditions of representation are such that they rob objects of the values they had at their first appearance to substitute the values they possess at their recurrence," George Santayana wrote in *Reason and Common Sense*. We can recognize the truth of this when we compare what the Constitution meant to the men of 1787 with what it meant to the Supreme Court in the first decades of our century, and again with what the clauses of the Constitution mean to us today. But it is equally true that in most cases in which our emotions are involved representation does not "rob objects" of their original values, but touches them with those original values on their repetition. So it is that when we become parents we try to build again the home we knew as children; the governor of a British colony tries to reproduce in miniature the forms and atmosphere of the Court of St. James's; the self-made man acts on the belief that his struggles and methods represent the one and only way to advancement.

It is the relevancy of experience to thought that distinguishes thought from paranoia; it is the testing of the idea by controlled experiment that distinguishes scientific thought from hunch or superstition. Consequently, education must fuse symbols with experience, if it is not to meander down the fatuous by-ways of scholasticism or breed an intellectual cinema of puppet-life, a veritable Hollywood romance played by beloved fantasies and freak misconceptions. We misunderstand so readily; we are so willing to be lured into daydreaming by pictures of promised lands or of the good old times. We found safety and satisfaction in our mother's arms and at various levels and in varying circumstances we want an all-star revival of that experience.

Of course, in the life of the infant, experience comes before symbols; facts and persons antedate the names by which they are called. Feeding precedes the bottle, which becomes a symbol of feeding. That is why early infantile experience is so persistent. It pervades not only complex chains of *symbols* through childhood and adult life, but also later experiences themselves. For later experiences are colored not only by the sensory imprint of first impressions, but by the symbols learned in infancy as well. A child may not understand such words as "the boss" or "work," but they are only partial abstractions because they are identified as related to "father." Thus the characters who participate in the family drama, the home which sets the scene and its furnishings, become symbols which are often unconsciously applied to other situations in later life and set the patterns for future behavior. Fathers and mothers, brothers and sisters live again and again in new relationships in homes of adult years, in employment, in social life and in church. "Let me be a sister to you," and "He is a father to me" are some of the many articulated examples of this truth.

As the child develops, he accumulates symbols and experiences, but at least until his formal education begins, there is likely to be an initial contact between symbol and experience itself. He does not have to deal much with the names of things not a part of his environment. Those strangers, "the boss" and "work," are an extension of father, like his newspaper, which is part of him too but which the child cannot understand. With his formal education, floodgates are opened and what he has learned through his faculties becomes inundated by words and numbers. Suddenly, symbols of things the like of which he has never known, must be learned through the medium of other symbols. Father's newspaper, which had been a daily repetition of ABC's, now becomes words, some of which have meaning. To make the initial school situation more difficult, if he has never been to nursery school or kindergarten, he must face these amazing new symbols in a period of emotional strain when he leaves the haven of home with its familiar rewards and punishments for the uncertainty of the classroom and the competition of contemporaries.

The first impact of school on child ought, then, to be accompanied by a clarification both of the new symbols and of new and old emotional stresses. It is through experience and attempting to attain physical skills that one gains mastery over the meaning of many symbols; and it is through the achievement of such security as experience and skill bring that nonintellectual doors are also opened. Consequently, doing is an important part of an education that is to have relevancy to living, if education is not to be but a sterile stimulant to those with a verbal cast of mind and a drudgery to all others.

From learning to handle his buttons in the nursery school and tools and materials in the elementary and early years of secondary schools to the scientific laboratory of the university, there are no limits to the young person's opportunities for doing. Nor should one omit physical education and sports conducted for sports' sake, (not a mere competition to win) from the doing skills to be experienced, if not mastered. It may not be practicable to build houses in every classroom, but every student can at least be made acquainted with some of the materials, processes and considerations that enter into house building, and his imagination constructing further with symbols will as a consequence have a more factual meaning. It may not be possible for every student to repeat all the experiments which have demonstrated scientific laws and indicated scientific hypotheses; but by performing some experiments he can get an understanding of the scientific method and an appreciation of the possibilities of objective thinking.

It is important, too, that the child be given the chance to learn the satisfaction of creating things and discovering things divorced from the satisfaction of his needs for reward and fears of punishment. The earlier the child can get such experience the better, for in the long run it is only by finding creative satisfactions (however personal, but better when shared with contemporaries) that the child will be freed from infancy and started on the route to maturity. The award of stars and prizes lulls teachers into thinking someone has learned something. Actually, all this defeats education in its broader aims, for it accentuates motivations brought about by rewards and punishments and defers, sometimes forever, the achievement of the capacity to do things because you can do them and like to do them and like to share your pleasure in the doing.

So the honest artist takes pleasure in the fact that someone else enjoys his creation and hopes that it will bring pleasure to others, but the work of art is not created with an anxious eye as to what the critics will say. The mature administrator, judge or legislator who is out to do a job well and not to enhance his own power, will try to meet issues frankly to obtain what he believes to be just and practical results, not primarily for a favorable headline and the praise of constituents, though these may follow. The competent teacher will be more interested in the development of her pupils than in their marks in competitive tests.

The infant learns not only the verbal language—that is, the symbols of its community—but also the emotional language of communion with others by means of aggression, escape, competition, co-operation, cruelty and love. Instinctively, it moves to its desired ends by means of the psychological weapon which it finds will bring it the desired goal or response or yield the quickest satisfaction of its real or fancied needs. Just as a full adult life requires contact between fact and symbol, so also is it necessary to a full adult life that there be a minimum of confusion between the real and fantastic ends which are sought. That is, not only must a word or a number relationship find ancestry in experience to have meaning, but for a mature satisfaction in life we must know the difference between our true purposes and the daydreams through which we tend to attain the unreachable and whitewash the unspeakable. Such contact between fact and symbol, such reduction to a minimum of confusions between real and fantastic ends, are necessary achievements, not only in personal life, but also in the life of a community and nation if it is to be democratic. So for a socially healthy climate, the destructive patterns of infancy must be skillfully or carefully discouraged and constructive patterns developed. Therefore, a dynamic school system must be alive to these necessities in the lives of individual pupils and in society as a whole.

If democracy is an adult enterprise, an adult way of living; if education in a democracy has the task of developing adults, then education cannot neglect the emotional life of young people, for it is emotional retardation and disorganization that frequently retards the healthy development of the mind and is frequently the basis of failure to achieve maturity. Temper tantrum, aggressive exhibitionism and terrified withdrawal are not escaped by adding 3 feet, 100 pounds and 20 years to our stature—they may continue to deprive the adult of adult satisfactions. This does not mean that the teacher should be a psychiatrist or fiddle with the emotional life of the child. But the teacher should be acquainted with fundamental principles of mental hygiene. And the life of the classroom should be such as to advance (rather than retard) emotional as well as intellectual maturity through encouraging successful achievement at the child's level of development, rather than imposing failure for his inability to meet an adult's arbitrary standard of what a child should achieve. One of the most persistent of these arbitrary standards is that what we learned or liked when we were young is what our children must learn and like. We hate to admit that we may have been misled or that our children are not little replicas of us.

A democratic school must rid the child of the fear of authority, which is basically a fear of parental authority transferred to the teacher, the principal and all other persons situated in a position of power with respect to the child. This does not mean that the teacher should belittle parents, but she should not foster authoritarian fears in school situations which bind upon childhood the fear of parents, a fear which, more frequently than one might suspect, blocks the expression of love of parents. In the name of creating respect for authority, teachers and parents tend at times to invoke fear. In biblical literature we see a change in the worshipers from the fear of God to the love of God. This change represents far more than a development in civilizations. It is also a pattern of desirable psychological progress in the individual, progress from fear of those in authority to respect for them. Through arbitrary discipline infantile patterns may be aggravated rather than diminished; and arbitrary discipline (though it may on occasion be necessary as a final resort) does not present a setting for co-operative effort or for any enterprise which develops a sense of common responsibility.

When one comes to an analysis of authority, what is it that children are generally to be "made" to respect? Is it not often only the humiliated pride of an inadequate or insecure adult that seeks to re-establish itself by demanding respect, which seeks a vision of virility through the symbol of causing a weaker person to bend the knee? The boy bends the knuckles of another boy and says, "Give up?" The adult in effect bends the knuckles of the child (or the child's emotional need of security) and says, "Give up?" This is what the Nazis have attempted to do to the churches in Germany, what the British have done in India, what the United States did forty years ago in the Philippines. It is what Calvin did in Geneva, Stalin in Moscow, the Inquisition in Spain. Is authority not too frequently a threat of retribution to the nonconformers?—or, intellectually, a last word with which to muffle nonconformist thought? Does a democratic people really want to have its children governed by fear, threats and repressions? Is that the respect for authority that we really want?

"You need to be disciplined," a father said to his child. "Do you know what discipline means?"—"Yes," she answered, "it means that you're stronger than I am." This is often all that discipline does mean; and even more frequently it is the child's reaction to the punishment which he deems unjust or incomprehensible. In such instances discipline misses its point. It teaches the lesson that the aggressor can have his way and that by measuring strength, i.e., through competition, he can get something worth while—because if you are strong enough in muscle or in the power to terrorize you can then, if you will, get your own way or destroy what you want to destroy. To a greater or less degree this has been the experience of most of us. In adult terms it represents the relation of the Prussian or Japanese father to his family, the imperialistic nation to those it dominates and in many instances of industry to its employees.

Respect for authority in a democratic situation requires

that the authority be not arbitrary, not emotional, not paternalistic, but understanding and understandable. Certainly this is the ambition of democracy as expressed in the boast that we are governed by law and not by men. The only authority to be respected is the authority that is itself respectful, and so in turn deserves respect. It is only by treating the child with respect that the child will respect himself and others, that he will be released from that fear of authority which makes democracies ineffectual and fattens autocrats. For example, Silone has pointed out in his *School for Dictators* Hitler's "fundamental notion that consent of the masses is always the result of the simultaneous employment of propaganda and violence." He plays, in other words, not merely on the deep, normal desire of the immature to find security in reliance on a great father-figure, but also on their simultaneous terror of this symbolic figure. All dictatorship is based on this infantile fantasy magnified to national or imperial dimensions.

From this we may also learn a lesson of how conquered nations should be treated. No matter how many German, Japanese and Italian ringleaders are executed, individual Germans, Japanese and Italians must be treated with respect. Authority will be all the more effective for being firm but neither patronizing nor brutal.

Again, if we are to have a democratic situation, information cannot be given to the child or to adults arbitrarily, *ex-cathedra*. This, too, is the technique, not of a people who are attempting to encourage respect each for the other but of dictatorship. The give and take of equals, of contemporaries, has educational values which a democracy requires. In the schools of a democracy, co-operative effort (between teacher and students as well as among students) should be encouraged because it leads to mutual respect and understanding. It frees the students from the fear that develops when authority says, "It *must* be so."

The most satisfactory creative effort is not only self-expression but a shared pleasure; and this satisfaction can never be imposed. The attitude of dictatorship is otherwise. To quote again from Silone:

> Everything a Fascist leader says must be presented under the irresistible guise of the obvious. "It is so because it is so, and it cannot be otherwise." All doubts are excluded and there is nothing to discuss.

The dynamics of fascism are rooted in the finality of the arbitrary; the dynamics of democracy in mutual respect and understanding, in dislike of or laughter at the arbitrary, and a denial that there is a final word. Sometimes the democratic method fails in school and in society, and in self-defense the community must act arbitrarily. But it is significant that in autocratic states, force is continually patrolling the streets or listening at keyholes, while as a general rule in democratic societies force hides behind the moral and propaganda values of popular opinion and the law.

Growth cannot be forced. The farmer knows this. He creates growing situations for his corn, he fertilizes and cultivates it, but the corn grows in its environment by reason of its own life processes. The farmer cannot pull the stalk by the tassel and say, "Grow now, damn you!" He cannot put manure on the field and resent the fact that the growth of the corn does not correspond with his desire. And so a teacher cannot toss classics at a child, whether they be Peter Rabbit or Aristotle, he cannot quote noble adages or moral precepts and say, "Learn now!" He cannot surround the child with teaching and expect growth to be at the rate and in the direction that he wants. Books and teaching can be at best conditions favorable to learning, to growing situations; they are sunlight, earth and fertilizer. But the learning and growing come inevitably out of a life process, and the climate of home and school can only encourage or frustrate the growth.

That is to say, learning and growing are not extraneous to the youngster, nor are they merely intellectual. We would not question the relevancy of physical growth to mental growth; adolescence is prerequisite to physical, emotional and mental maturity. There is no longer reason to doubt the influence of emotional development on mental growth. Neither the sound mind nor sound body can be realized where emotions remain infantile. Certainly infantile emotions cannot lead to stable social organization in a democratic world.

We now say that children learn through the hand as well as through eye and ear; but it is also true that they learn through the emotions. Parents and teachers may express interest in the child, but the child knows through his emotions whether that interest is formal or genuine, whether it is such as to give him security and build-up or whether, in reality, it is ignoring him. This is brought out by the story of the child who was building a skyscraper of kindergarten blocks. "Look," he said to his teacher. She looked and said, "Uh, huh." And the child said, "You say

'Uh, huh' and look. Mama says 'Uh huh' but she don't look." A child learns through his emotions faster than through the intellect the discrepancies that exist between word and fact, and the extent of his own power over others, whether exercised by affection, docility or tantrum. Angel and brat are components of every child and contain the nuclei of the humane and the vicious adult.

It is not only the attitude—that is, the approach—of the educational system, but also the activity involved in the schooling which is important in resolving emotional conflicts, in bringing the population from the infantile level to the adult, in civilizing the young "barbarians." Intellectualism, sophistication, throwing down the old barriers are not sufficient. For the sophisticated debauchery and brilliant cruelty of such a period as the Renaissance are no more suitable to democracy than the semi-civilized purges and terrors of Stalinist Russia. In neither instance can the mass of the people achieve maturity. In neither circumstance could the schools—even if permitted to make the attempt—provide an atmosphere or activities to develop balanced personalities.

The schools of a democracy in the earliest years of the child's education, in nursery school and kindergarten, must afford him an opportunity of externally dramatizing through his play the dramas which are surging within him, which are emotionally the most important thing in his life. Later, through arts and crafts, sports and the symbolic expression of the written and spoken word, children must be afforded new opportunities for dramatization of their emotional problems; they must be encouraged to release those emotions, rather than discouraged. For *this* purpose it is unimportant whether the skills acquired are technically sound or whether the knowledge sought is or is not co-ordinated, so long as it answers some fundamental need of the child. It is only through the resolution of such needs, through the attainment of maturity, that a sound base for technical achievement and digested knowledge can be established, that that independent, self-reliant character which is at the foundation of democratic citizenship can be achieved.

Children are the more educable because their behavior patterns have been less congealed than those of adults; and, too, because while they are learning and meeting new situations and new concepts which may bring anxiety in their *entourage*, they can usually find security in the love and interest of their parents. Threatening new situations and ideas cannot be met by adults with the same means of reassurance but only through a fellowship based on equality. Anxieties can be quieted by reciprocal acceptance. This is the psychological response which causes men and women under bombardment to forego their differences and merge their interests. But the hardening of competitive patterns and set loyalties and identifications makes it difficult to modify the attitudes of adults.

Although the possibilities of education for adults are less fundamental than for children, adult education will become increasingly important. It does give an opportunity to many people to develop their capacities and to gain skills, understanding, pleasure and self-assurance. After the war adult education must be adapted to the needs of millions of young people throughout the world who were interrupted in their education by the calls of the war. In the conquered countries the new education must be instituted to attempt to modify the attitudes of adults as well as children towards each other and towards people who differ from them. It must aim to give them means of expression which will relieve them of inevitable hates and terrors and thus break the cycle leading to renewed hostility and aggression.

In occupied lands, too, education dare not return to its academic patterns. Propaganda and suffering will have twisted the emotions of young and old. Feeding, clothing and pacifying the world and making it creative in the arts of peace will not of themselves make a safe or satisfactory world. These are, besides being material goods, possible curricular materials for education of the emotions towards social and moral ends. How to exploit such possibilities should be the immediate task of an international education office.

Of course, if one is not interested in democratic citizenship, all the preceding discussion can be ignored. A Hitler and his henchman, a pyramiding financier and his satellites, can be content with skillful engineers, technicians, clever lawyers and propagandists prepared to sell their techniques for ready cash, or a slap on the back, or just to be hailed as a good fellow. But such ideologies defy the basic needs of human beings and the fundamental fact of democratic society—that it is an enterprise depending upon an emotionally mature population, motivated by a desire to share and co-operate rather than to truckle or destroy. Without the guiding moral principle that the aim of society is to achieve respect for every individual and equal opportunity for his full development as a creative and social being, education for skills and training in techniques and cleverness is education for prostitution to autocracy or wealth.

What we want from our schools and what we must work for in our schools are three things: the mastery of the meaning of those symbols and of that experience which we call culture; the acquisition of competency in those skills which give satisfaction or vocation or both; and the attainment of emotional stability and balance. These are three facets all essential to education for democratic citizenship. It is through such education that there can be wrought the foundations of the democratic faith.

If we are serious in our talk of ethical and democratic social ends, we must understand that words and institutions are not to be taken at their face values, but in terms of the human values behind them. Something stimulates us to speak—something stimulates us to create and maintain and destroy social organisms. What are the drives that cause men to seek what we call democratic society and to support what we call democratic institutions? What are the drives, conscious and unconscious, which are antagonistic to the realization of such a society and such institutions? We have been blind to these questions long enough. So long as we ignore psychological patterns of behavior, we shall with shocked naïveté or sadistic pleasure repeatedly encounter periods in which destructive forces come into headlong conflict with democratic goals and threaten all the progress that men have made for centuries towards the fulfillment of their desire to achieve ethical ends and the satisfaction of their instinctive need for a recognition of individual integrity.

We have seen that the fundamental human patterns, which underlie our lives from nursery to the inner councils of industry and politics and form that composite, plaid pattern which we know of as society, include at least these tendencies and needs: (1) A tendency to seek dominion over others in order to quiet anxieties of insufficiency. (2) A tendency to preserve dominion over others—to maintain a paternalistic relationship. (3) A tendency to attempt to gain equality in order to obtain freedom from paternalism—or to attempt to complete the fantasy of an all-powerful father-figure. (4) A tendency to confuse equality with identity—to find anxiety in differences, to feel cheated if identical treatment is not extended. (5) A tendency to attempt to compel identity in others because of an implied threat when it is necessary to measure ourselves, our achievements or ambitions against others. (6) A need to find security in acceptance by others, in the development of our capacities and the sharing with others of experiences and the fruits of those capacities. (7) A need to find security in self-reliance and collaboration rather than in a search for power or reward from those in power—security in brotherhood rather than in competition.

These, together with problems set for us by the physical world, are the real objects to which the political sciences must address themselves. The others are fantasies or symptoms. The maladjustments of political institutions, of economic practices, of social relationships, of educational curricula are the fevers and the rashes of society. Their adjustment depends not upon patching them up, not upon fiddling with their machinery as much as upon understanding the maladjustments of the human beings behind them and guiding people to healthy maturity.

When I was a boy I had a penny bank with a globe of the world on top of it, and every time a penny was dropped in, the globe spun around. Beneath was the motto, "Money makes the world go round." But does it? The answer to this question must be determined by one's attitude. If you believe that it is important to make the world go round or that it is money that makes it go round, then you will find in weapons and institutions, in aggression and subservience, in paternalism and domination the way of life. But if not, then you will address yourself to finding a way to help people free themselves from those anxieties which produce paternalism, which deny equality, which demand identical treatment and behavior, which drive people to competition and aggression and to seek dominion over others. It is the choice between the approach of politics and the approach of ethics and science. Only when politics serves ethical ends and satisfies the mature needs of man can political institutions assure men the freedom to be free.

Acknowledgments

THE AUTHOR wishes to make acknowledgment to the Viking Press for permission to quote from *Wayward Youth*, by August Aichhorn; to Harper & Brothers for permission to quote from *School for Dictators*, by Ignazio Silone; to World Peace Foundation for permission to quote from *The Far East: An International Survey*, by Harold S. Quigley and George Hubbard Blakeslee; to Random House for permission to quote from *Poems: 1925-1940*, by Louis MacNeice; and to George H. Sabine and the Cornell University Press for permission to quote from Mr. Sabine's edition of *Law of Freedom* by Gerrard Winstanley.

The following chapters of this book originally appeared in magazines: "Competitive Society" in *Mental Hygiene*; "Plato's Sea Captain and Buddha's Navel" in *Harper's*; and "Man Cannot Live by Words Alone" published by the Progressive Education Association.

Index

Abel, 60, 62-63, 65
Abelard and Héloïse, 241
Adams, Henry, 4-5
Adler, Mortimer, 237
Administrative boards, 110-11, 140
Adolescence, 40, 44-46, 69-70, 124, 173, 263; social, 52-58
Adult education, 265-66
Agriculture, 18-19
Agriculture, Department of, 114, 128-29
Aichhorn, August, 165-66, 174
Alsace Lorraine, 155
Anglo-Saxon, hundreds, 123
Anglo-Saxons, 146
Aquinas, Thomas, 224, 229, 241, 245
Arabs, 207
Aristocracy, 49, 226-27, 234
Aristotle, 88, 117, 126, 226-29, 233-34, 241
Asquith, H. H., 154
Athens, 97, 226, 233
Atlantic Charter, 185
Attila the Hun, 146
Augustine, *City of God*, 87
Australia, 154
Austria, 153-54

Bacon, Francis, 229
Balkans, 202-04, 209
Bavaria, 206
Belgium, 202
Benes, Edouard, 206, 210
Bentham, Jeremy, 106
Bernard, Claude, 1, 119-20
Bernhardi, F. A. J. von, 151
Bible, 60, 62, 72
Biddle, Nicholas, 30
Bismarck, Otto E. L. von, 151-54, 157, 203

Boxer Rebellion, 188
Brecht, Arnold, 217
Buddha, 84, 158, 228-29
Bulgaria, 210
Burke, Edmund, 28-29
Burma, 205

Cain, 60-63
Calvin, John, 131, 260
Calvinism, 148
Canada, 214
Canossa, 148
Capitalism, 24-26, 30-35, 37, 139, 156, 198-99; medieval, 24; state, 34-35, 138-39
Carlyle, A. J., 88
Carr, Cecil Thomas, 124-26
Cartels, 27, 135
Catholic Church, 72-73
Catholics, 44, 57
Cavour, Count di, 204
Charlemagne, 147
Chiang Kai-shek, 189
Child labor, 19
China (-ese), 158, 160-61; Communism, 178, 192; co-operatives, 136; Philosphy, 66; postwar, 177, 188, 192; Western imperialism, 161
Cicero, 88
City managers, 109
Civil rights, 102-03
Clan society, 48-49, 54, 61-62, 71
Classical learning, 223-46
Claustrophobia, 194
Clemenceau, Georges, 175
Cleveland, Grover, 108
Collaboration, 3, 84, 268; international, 218-19
Communism, 25, 58, 99, 171, 178, 187, 192, 213

271

Competition, free, 19, 27, 31, 37-41; aggressive, 63-64; growth away from, 90
Competitive society, 60-78
Confucius, 84, 158
Congress of Industrial Organizations, 115
Constant, Benjamin, 149
Constitution, United States, 95, 98, 113, 211, 253
Contract, free, 19, 26-27, 29, 35, 39-40
Cooke and Murray, 133
Co-operation, 35, 89, 116, 184-85, 257; in education, 261; international, 208-14
Co-operatives, 131, 135-41, 168; unifying force, 212-13, 218
Co-operative society, 108
Copernicus, Nikolaus, 230
Corporation taxes, wartime, 18
Corporations, 132
Corporative state, 17
Cromwell, Oliver, 57, 95-96, 148, 178
Crop allotments, 18
Cynics, 92
Czechoslovakia, 205, 206

Danube Commission, 212-13
Danzig, 210
Darwinism, 99
David, Kingdom of, 64, 205
Declaration of Independence, 82, 87, 98
Democracy, 17, 189; alternative to paternalism, 128-41; definitions of, 83, 99-104; drives for and against, 267; dynamics of, 94, 99-100, 134, 262; education for, 232-69; fear of, 94-95; Greek concept of, 97; ideology of, 232; inner threat to, 5; maturity necessary to, 58-59, 266; new forms, 116, 128, 140-41; principles of, assumptions, 3, 83-86, 90; propagation of, 223-69; Protestantism, 148; relationships, problem of, 67-68; test for health of, 108, 109
Denmark, co-operative in, 135

Depersonalization, of institutions, 73; of religion, 72
Descartes, René, 229
Dewey, John, 5, 21, 41, 115, 121
Dictators, 91, 99, 246, 261-62
Dictatorship, 87, 123-24
Diderot, Denis, 29
Difference, see Variation
"Digger" pamphlets, 50
Dissenters, coercion of, 99-101
Dutch, see Netherlands

Ebert, Fritz, 156
Edman, Irwin, 85
Education, adult, 265-66; in citizenship, 244-45; classical, 233-46; co-operative effort, 261-62; for democracy, 220-21, 232-69; doing as part of, 255-57; emotional life, developing, 258-65, 267; three objectives, 267
Education office, international, 218, 266
Education, vocational, see Vocational education
Einstein, Albert, 145
Emotions, learning through, 263-64, 267
Encirclement, 194
Equality, 3, 37-59, 84, 139, 182, 191, 265, 268; Aristotle vs. Cicero and Seneca, 88; in clan, 48-50; concept of, 66, 84; democratic expression, 128; in family pattern, 66-68; humanizing, 40; of opportunity, 247; psychological roots, 59; of races, 185-87, 191-93; in religious faiths, 46-47, 85-86; struggle for, 50-58
Equity vs. power, 48
Equivalence, 42, 46
Esau, 61-63, 65
Experts, 106, 107; administration by, 74-75, 120-21; increased power of, 113-16; in government and industry, 136-40; relation to public, 116-29, 140
Export-Import Bank, 112

Fact finding, 120
Factory system, 32, 34, 108, 110

Index

Family, 42-45, 77; pattern of, 66-71, 152-54, 163-64, 172-73, 260-61; ethical, 66-69
Fascism, 17, 25, 132; dynamics of, 262
Father-image, 53-56, 61-62, 123-24, 152-53, 163-64, 172, 260
Federalist, The, 95, 98, 113
Federal Reserve System, 107, 110-11
Federation, 208, 209; world, 217-19
Feudalism, 58, 73, 77, 234; manor, 250; passing of, 197, 238
Fichte, Johann G., 145, 150, 218
Finance capitalism, 32
Financiers, 17-18, 75
Ford, Henry, 34
Fortune, 27
France, 148-49, 155-56, 182, 203, 205; Empire, 216; Revolution, 22, 37, 73, 148, 157, 178
France, Banque de, 30
Francis, St., 84
Franciscans, 160
Franklin, Benjamin, 116
Franks, 147
Fraternity, 37-38, 59, 131; drive toward, 89; international, 212, 220-21
Frederick the Great, 149, 157
Frederick William I, 149
Free Cities, 98
Freedoms, four, 102-03
Freud, Sigmund, 241
Freudians, 54
Fusion movements, 109

Galileo, 230
Gandhi, 2, 93, 103
Gaul, 146
General Board of Health, Great Britain, 110
Gens or clan, 48-49
Germans, 57
Germany, 8, 203, 205, 209; aggressor, 194-95; delinquency, 143-58; family pattern, 152-54, 172-73, 260; history, 146-58; nationalism, 193; Nazi revolution, 17, 166-68, 172, 175; paternalism, 169-70, 173; postwar, United Nations program for, 168-77, 179-80; revolution, possibility of, 167, 170; self-sufficiency, 196
Goethe, Johann Wolfgang von, 145
Gold, 17
Golden and Ruttenberg, 99-100, 134
Grants in aid, 111
Great Britain, 8, 17, 95-98, 131, 153, 156, 203, 205, 234; Constitution, 211; co-operatives, 135; Empire, 57, 216; fascism, 25; grants in aid, 111; imperialism, 185-88, 191-92, 260; laborers, statute of, 18; maturity, 58-59; national unity, 148; Navy, 202, 203, 205; Poor Law Board and Board of Health, 110; Revolution, 73, 157, 178; self-sufficiency, 197; social insurance, 154; social service state, 74; wartime taxes, 18-19
Great Elector, 149, 158
Greece, 209; city-states, 205; democracy, 97, 99; drama, 62; experts, problem of, 117; Periclean Age, 223-24
Greeks, 45, 87, 223-24, 226-27, 230, 232
Gregory VII, Pope, 147-48
Guilds, 24, 98, 129-30

Hailie Selassie, 205
Hamilton, Alexander, 95
Have-nots, 95
Hegel, G. W. F., 151-52, 217-18
Heine, Heinrich, 145, 150
Henry IV, 147-48
Hideyoshi, 160
Hindus, 228, 249
Hinkle, Beatrice, 151
Hirohito, 178-79
Hitler, Adolf, 8, 25, 124, 147, 154, 157, 165-68, 175, 205, 210, 261; *Mein Kampf*, 57, 152-53
Holy Roman Emperors, 147
Homer, 229
Hoover, Herbert, 20
Huguenots, 148
Hull trade agreements, 198

Human nature, 183; fatalistic view of, 183; possibilities for development, 184-87
Hungary, 205, 208, 209

Identity, 3, 42-44, 46, 53, 67, 84, 86-88, 90, 182, 268
Ihering, Rudolf von, 138-39
Imperialism, 161, 185-88, 191-92, 260
Income taxes, 18, 107, 110-11
India, 58, 188, 191-92, 260
Individualism, rugged, 40
Individuals, 3, 34, 40, 47-48; democratic assumptions concerning, 84-86; society, relation to, 68-78, 90; variations, 84, 90
Industrial revolution, 28, 32, 116
Industry, authoritarian attitude, 132-34, 260; centralization, 114-116; need for labor voice, 132-34
Industry Committee, 128
Industry Council, 134
Inflation, 156, 198
Inheritance taxes, 18-19
International Bureau of Weights and Measures, 211
International Copyright Union, 211
International Labor Office, 211, 213, 218
Internationals, First and Second Socialist, 213
International Telegraph Union, 211, 213
Interstate Commerce Commission, 110
Iraq, 207
Ireland, 57-58
Italy, 17, 204, 205, 209; aggressor attitude, 194-95; nationalism, 193

Jacob, 48, 61-63, 65, 102
Japan, 8, 44, 182, 205; aggressor attitude, 194; delinquency, 158-80; family pattern, 260; feudalism, 159, 161-64; 177-78, 193, 204; Mikado, 159, 163-64; paternalism, 164; revolution, possibility of, 178; *Samurai,* 159-65, 178, 188; self-sufficiency, 196

Jefferson, Thomas, 98, 106, 108, 109, 116, 187, 245
Jesuits, 160
Jesus, 72, 84
Jews, 44, 81, 91, 158, 168, 228-29; commonwealth, 206, 207, 209
Joseph, 48, 91, 102
Junkers, 156
Justice vs. power, 48
Justinian Code, 229

Kant, Emmanuel, 150, 218
Korea, 158, 160

Labor, 17-18, 32, 34, 114-15, 130, 134, 141, 154
Labor Relations Board, 18
Labor unions, *see* Unions
Lafayette, Marquis de, 187
Laissez faire, 105, 113, 115, 140
Lamas of Lhasa, 165, 229
Lao-tse, 84
Latin America, 99, 191, 203
Lattimore, Owen, 189
League of Nations, 99, 182, 215-17
Lenin, 57, 124, 156
Liberalism, 19, 26, 37
Liebknecht, Karl, 156
Lindbergh, Anne, 145
Livy, 229
Loans and credits, government, 17-18
Local government, 108-10, 122-23; enfeeblement, 112, 140; new forms, 128-29, 140-41
Locke, John, 151, 230
London, City of, 17
Louisiana Purchase, 108
Luther, Martin, 147-48
Luxemburg, Rosa, 156

Machiavelli, Niccolò, 229
McIlwain, C. H., 87
Madison, James, 106, 113
Maimonides, 229
Majority rule, 81, 83, 99-102
Managerial revolution, 116
Mann, Thomas, 144
Marcus Aurelius, 85

Index

Marshall, Lenore G., 194
Marx, Karl, 151, 218
Marxism, 6, 25-26, 65, 138, 245
Maturity, achievement of, 45-46, 51-59, 63-66, 256-57, 264-65; program for, 78; of colored peoples, 187; of common man, 54; in home, 67, 90; psychological factors in, 59, 78, 84, 91-92
Mead, Margaret, 24-25
Medicine man, 48, 50
Mercantilism, 32, 37, 116, 197
Merriam, C. E., 112-13
Mexico, farm labor, 200
Middle Ages, 77, 228
Mill, John Stuart, 124-25
Minorities, 208-11
Moltke, H. K. B. von, 151
Monopoly, 19, 27-28, 31-34, 65, 105
Moors, in Spain, 228
Morgan (J. P.) and Company, 18
Morgan, Lewis H., 49
Moses, 84
Murray, Philip, 134
Mussolini, Benito, 25, 45, 124, 196

Napoleon, 123-24, 149, 167, 187
Napoleon III, 153, 167
National Association of Manufacturers, 94
Nationalism, 193, 207
Nationality, Soviet Principle of, 193
Nations, conflicts of, 77; co-operation between, 208-14; federation, 208, 209; occupied, re-education, 266; small, 202-08; sovereignty, 204, 211-12; variations, 209-11; wayward, 142-80
Nazism, 184, 247-48, 260
Negroes, 44, 81, 98
Nehru, Jawaharlal, 143
Netherlands, 186, 191-92, 202
New Deal, 113, 154
New England, town meeting, 97, 123
New Zealand, 136, 154
Nietzsche, F. W., 145, 150
Norris-La Guardia Act, 18
NRA, 129

Oligarchy, 97; of experts, 121, 126-27, 140

Palestine, 207
Parliamentary state, 26-28, 31
Paternalism, 47, 51-54, 71, 74-77, 88, 153, 169-70, 173, 185; of employer, 128, 130, 154; in family, see Family; international, 216, 219-21; labor, 130-31; new, 117, 140; patterns of, 62; political, 90-94, 116; social, 52-54; of technicians, 119; revolt against, 36, 47, 89, 104
Patriarch, 48-50
Paul, St., 66
Pax Britannica, 38, 203
Philippines, 192, 260
Planning, government, 17-20, 31; by experts, 120
Plato, 226-27, 229, 234; *Laws*, 223-24; Republic, 95
Plotinus, 227
Poincare, Raymond, 175
Poland, 90-91, 158, 174, 205-07
Poll tax, 98
Poor Law Board, Great Britain, 110
Power, drive for, 50, 61-65; fallacy of, 66; guilt of, 62; vs. justice, 48; loss of, 54-55; reason for quest, 182-83; uses and abuses of, 6-9
Prices, control of, 19-20
Primogeniture, law of, 50
Produce exchanges, 17
Production line, 32
Profit motive, 71, 139
Property, 39, 49-50; family relationship to, 67; as power, 55; rights, 27-30, 33
Protestantism, 148
Prussia, 106, 148-49, 151, 153, 206, 260
Prussians, 57
Psychological patterns of behavior, 4-9, 26, 51, 267-69
Puritans, 56, 73, 157, 178
Putney debates, 95

Quakers, 66, 74, 102

Quigley and Blakeslee, 162

Rathenau, Walter, 156
Raw materials, 30, 32, 185-86, 198
Realpolitik, 202, 213
Recognition, desire for, 70-72, 86, 91-92, 128
Reconstruction Finance Corporation, 20, 110-12
Reformation, 72
Renaissance, 264
Revolutionists, group solidarity, 55-56
Revolutions, American, 22, 37, 73, 157, 178, 197; democratic, current, 13-36, 53-54; French, 22, 37, 73, 148, 157, 178; postwar, 187-88; Puritan, English, 73, 157, 178; Russian, 16-17, 178-79; Spartacist, 156
Ricardo, David, 29
Rights of Man, Declaration of, 87
Robespierre, Maximilien de, 37, 57
Rochdale, co-operative, 135
Roman Empire, 146-47, 216
Romans, 87
Rome, Church of, 146-48
Roosevelt, Franklin D., 2, 83
Rousseau, Jean Jacques, 50, 214
Rumania, 209
Russia, see Union of Socialist Soviet Republics

Samurai, 145, 159-65, 178
Santayana, George, 253
Saxons, 147
Schopenhauer, Arthur, 145
Scotland, 131, 203
Seagle, William, 123-24
Securities Exchange Commission, 17
Self-determination, 204
Shinto religion, 158
Silone, Ignazio, 108-09, 261-62
Skills, 255-56, 267
Slavery, 49
Smith, Adam, 106, 115-16
Smith, Alfred E., 137
Smoot-Hawley Tariff Act, 198
Social security, 154-55
Social service state, 74, 110-14, 128-29

Society, ethical ends of, 84-86; individual and, 68-78, 86
Socrates, 84
Sovereignty, national, 204, 211-12
Spain, 205, 228, 260
Spartacist Revolution, 156, 187
Spinoza, Baruch, 230
Stalin, Joseph, 8, 57, 124, 156, 167, 171, 260
Stock exchanges, 17
Stoics, 66, 84-85
Sudetenland, 210
Suffrage, universal, 39
Sugar Commission, 212
Sun Yat-sen, 188
Supreme Court, 19, 115, 253
Sweden, 135, 205
Switzerland, 205, 209
Symbols, 249-55, 257
Syria, 207

Tacitus, 229
Talleyrand, 187
Tariffs, 39, 113, 198-99
Tariff unions, 214
Technological age, 41
Tennessee legislature, 99
Tennessee Valley Authority, 136
Thailand, 205
Thirty Years' War, 148, 167
Thoreau, Henry D., 100-01
Tocqueville, Alexis de, 117-18
Totalitarianism, 17, 23, 35, 47-48
Town meeting, 97, 123
Trans-Jordan, 207
Translyvanians, 209
Trotsky, Leon, 57

Unemployment, 27, 33
Union of Socialist Soviet Republics, 8, 135, 140, 171, 192, 203, 205, 211, 217, 264; nationality, principle of, 193; postwar, 187; Revolution, 16-17, 178-79; self-sufficiency, 196-97
Unions, labor, 72, 99-100, 110, 128, 130-35, 139, 157, 212-13
United Nations, 219

Index

United States, co-operatives, 136; imperialism, 161, 185-88; middle class, 156; and Latin Americans, 203; Social service state, 74, 110-14, 128-29
Universal Postal Union, 211
Utilitarians, 38-39

Variation, 3, 42-46, 51, 55, 63, 66, 69-70, 84, 90-92, 186, 200, 268; between nations, 209-11
Versailles, Treaty of, 155, 186, 210, 216
Vocational education, 224-26, 231, 233, 238, 242

Wages and Hours Act, 18, 128
Wagner Act, 13, 18
Wagner, Richard, 145
Wall Street, 17, 20, 27
Weimar Republic, 156, 167
Wells, H. G., 161
Wilhelm II, Kaiser, 147, 154, 196
Wilson, Woodrow, 99, 106, 107, 123, 125, 182
Winstanley, Gerrard, 50
Wordsworth, William, 90
Works Progress Administration, 155

Zionism, 206, 207
Zweig, Arnold, 144-45